A MEAL OBSERVED

A Meal Observed

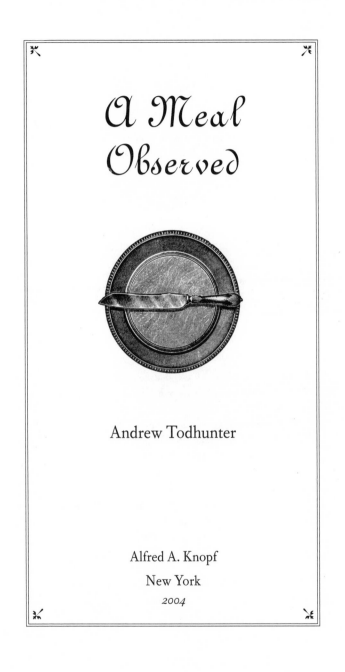

Andrew Todhunter

Alfred A. Knopf

New York

2004

Library of Congress Cataloging-in-Publication Data
Todhunter, Andrew.
A meal observed / Andrew Todhunter.
p.   cm.
ISBN 0-375-41085-6
1. Cookery, French. 2. Dinners and dining. I. Title.
TX719.T58 2004
641.5944—dc21
2003056186

Manufactured in the United States of America
First Edition

For my parents

Contents

L'Arrivée

I park at the corner of the rue Balzac and the Avenue de Friedland, and the instant I cut the engine I become aware that I am nervous. Performance anxiety, butterflies, a mild version of the racking nerves I used to suffer, as a freshman and sophomore in high school, before a wrestling match. The fear that I would be humiliated, outmanned, before the eyes of my coach, my teammates, and a girl whose name I had shoveled in the snow, on the frozen Hudson River, in letters visible to passing aircraft. In the car, I glance quickly over at my wife, who smiles gamely but a little uncomfortably, and we sit for a long moment in silence, not moving, in a kind of feigned, mutual optimism, as if bracing for embarrassing news. I try not to think it through, because I know that analysis will only make it worse, and that I am here, *we* are here, to enjoy ourselves. I glance at the car clock, then my watch, and their unexpected synchronicity provides a flush of paramilitary satisfaction. I slip my cell phone out of the inside breast pocket of my jacket and check the time in the upper right-hand corner of its miniature screen. All three! A good omen, and proof, despite the state of my front bumper, creased into an awkward V against a black Mercedes' tow bar in Brugge, that my equipment and I are essentially on the ball. According to these three chronometers, it is 8:15 in the evening on Tuesday, July 13, 1999, the eve of Bastille Day. We are early.

I glance again at my wife. Erin is thirty-two and beautiful—stunning, really—and for this I'm grateful. Her beauty is the one sure thing we have on this world we are about to enter, the thing no waiter or sommelier or *maître d'hôtel* at Taillevent—a Michelin three-star restaurant considered by many critics to be the finest in France and thus the world—can wrest from us with a patronizing glance. In hours of need, one can remind oneself that beauty, more even than youth, its reckless twin, has ever been a fortune before which wealth, sophistication, and intellect will bow.

We are also prepared to spend between twenty-five hundred and three thousand francs—four to five hundred dollars out of our own pockets—on a meal for two. This is something we have never done. Not only because we are often nearly penniless, given the vicissitudes of my work, but because we are not, truly, gourmands. By and large, that is not where our money goes. For reasons fiscal, temperamental, and psychological, we eat out rarely, and when we do we often bring it home. Furthermore, though we have bought the odd issue of *Gourmet* or *Saveur,* we have not yet subscribed to such magazines. We are not, in short, "foodies." I object to the very word "foodie," not only for its inherent ugliness as a sound, but for its cliquishness. "I'm a *huge* foodie," a woman told me recently at a dinner party, with that mixture of false shame and childlike enthusiasm that accompanies nearly any public revelation of sensual preference, and it struck me as surprisingly intimate, even indecent, as if this near-stranger had slipped off her Roman sandals, stretched her calves across my lap, and asked if I would like to eat her feet. I later admitted that if this particular foodie had been more attractive her confession might not have troubled me. In that case, it might well have conjured the agreeable image of her nude and reclining in a bathtub of mashed banana.

Our status as nonfoodies notwithstanding, my wife and I both like to cook, and even more we like to sit and eat at a comfortable table for long hours. And that is one reason we are here, at this moment, at the corner of Balzac and Friedland. For there are few moments more existentially harmonious than those that make up the latter half of a good meal in a hospitable restaurant, in the company of one or two people—rarely more— with whom one feels almost entirely safe, and by whom one feels at least partially understood. I had such a meal at an underrated one-star restaurant named Julien, in Strasbourg, on the quai des Bateliers, with my wife and her mother some six years ago. By some turn of fate for which I shall always be grateful, I have been blessed with a mother-in-law who is excellent company. I would never have imagined, as a bachelor, that I might take some of the best trips in my life with my wife *and* her mother, but there it is. The fact that she is a good deal younger than we are in spirit certainly helps, and there is always the vague sense that we are traveling with a mysteriously greying niece. In any case, the near-perfection of such a meal has less to do with the food, with the procession of well-wrought dishes, than with that gathering condition of *bien-être* induced by wine and victuals and companionship in a warm, preferably unfamiliar setting, all the while under the care of sure-handed and anonymous strangers.

This state generally peaks late in the evening, and usually at the pause when the dinner plates have been cleared away. There is first of all the caloric high, the rush of blood sugar, the false sensation that all is well in the world because one has eaten well. The conversation usually peaks at this time, and everyone at the table is giddy. At that moment, a server often brushes the tablecloth. The conversation at a pause, you may lean back away from the table to admire this orderly gesture. You may be struck by the suspicion that Western civilization, beleaguered by greed, cynicism, and bad taste, might simply be preserved through the observance of this solitary act. When the server withdraws, you luxuriate in the sight of the freshly cleaned white tablecloth, minutely spotted here and there, perhaps, but smooth and free of crumbs, and as you lean back in, resting your forearms on the table, you sweep the white expanse with an open palm. The candlelight soaks into the cloth, and glimmers on the surviving silverware, and the white noise of the other conversations in the restaurant is decorous but lively. You feel as if you are swimming unseen in the well of these voices, through these foreign and contented lives. Besotted with this confluence of nurture and sedation, free of fear and responsibility, you stare blankly at the cloth, or up into the flame of the candle, or close your eyes and sink into the taste and heat of the wine, into the womblike center of these concentric human circles, one within another within another—and for a moment you will know that you are here, truly here, at *this* table in *this* restaurant in *this* benign and generous world.

If one has been careful with the wine, but not too careful, the afterglow of this rapture *de la table* can last well into the drive home, and even, if you hurry, into bed.

The anonymity of the waiter is in itself important, and serves a number of functions. In America, of course, to global ridicule, we have made the widespread mistake of training our servers to introduce themselves to their customers by name. This has not yet trickled down into the kind of rural American diner frequented by deer hunters, where the waitress might reflexively call you "hon" but will have far too much common sense than to burden you with her identity. It is largely for this reason that I like such diners, where, when you've dulled your senses to the fence of neon-orange vests along the counter, and the fraternal "I'm gonna kill me an animal" intention that hangs in the air like the scent of sawdust and sour beer, you can still get a fine breakfast of eggs, hash browns, toast, and coffee for under five bucks.

I should confess that, though I am willing to catch or spear fish, I haven't eaten red meat in some years, and feel viscerally opposed to terrestrial sport-hunting for reasons I can't quite articulate. My paternal grandfather was a fanatical hunter and fly fisherman, and my father likes to fish from time to time, so I have no doubt that I would enjoy everything about big-game hunting except gunning the animals down. In fact, I could well imagine spending hours or days in pursuit of a large animal with an empty rifle, if only to draw a perfect bead on it— De Niro at the end of *The Deer Hunter*—and let the animal pass. My mother, for her part, spontaneously became an ovolactovegetarian at age six. I believe it happened at breakfast, when she declared she would not eat the bacon on her plate, or any other meat for that matter, as long as she lived. This was in 1932, when Americans who chose not to eat meat were considered not merely odd but dangerously out of their minds. Nearly seventy years later, she has yet to wriggle out of this vow. If I inherited a portion of my grandfather's love of sport, and a portion of my mother's sensibility regarding animals, spear fishing may represent some kind of lame behavioral compromise. When I was a young boy in New England, the day I came ashore with my first speared rockfish and cleaned them on a stump at a friend's house, the smell of fresh blood on my hands triggered an unexpected and primordial response. I rubbed the blood up and down my forearms, painting them, and nearly swooned from its sight and its sweet sticky smell. It was powerfully arousing in some un-cultured way, and I might easily have smeared the rest of my eight-year-old body with the blood had I not felt some shame in my excitement. Later, I experienced a measure of revulsion when it came time to eat the thick white meat of the fried fish that I had speared, although I forced myself to eat it, and that feeling rarely recurred. Now I spearfish much more rarely, and when I do I feel a bit sorrier for the fish. It has also been quite some time since I was excited by the smell and sight of blood, and even longer since I felt a pang of revulsion at eating the flesh of an animal so recently living.

My father, who taught me to fish, taught me to kill them quickly, to reduce unnecessary suffering, and I had assumed this was a universal practice. One summer dusk in New England, however, my father and I came across a man casting for bluefish; a huge blue lay on the sand, gulping and flapping. "Aren't you going to kill it?" I asked the man. "No need," he answered over his shoulder, "it'll die on its own." I watched the fish struggle and wondered if there was some way I could kill it, as was proper, without causing offense. I saw no way around the problem, and finally my father and I said good night to the fisherman and moved along.

In any case, the anonymity of the waiter helps first to define what is an ancient, respectable, and specific relationship. The waiter, when he is your waiter, is not Jonathan. He is not a married father of two with a bad knee and a gambling habit. He is in possession of greater or lesser amounts of grace, charm, skill, knowledge, warmth, and decorum, but he is your waiter, and should remain nameless. Of course, the American waiter who takes his or her job seriously is a rare thing.

My impeccably mannered sister-in-law recently asked a Californian waiter in an Italian restaurant, confidentially, if it was indeed true that chefs dreaded orders for zabaglione, the labor-intensive concoction of egg yolks, sugar, and Marsala wine. A skilled waiter might have produced any number of informative, amusing, and tip-leavening responses to such an inquiry, but this fellow replied flatly, "Now, *that's* a stupid question." I wasn't there, but I'm sure they knew his name.

More objectionable still than "Hi, my name is Jonathan . . ." is the phrase to follow. After the opening introduction, the waiter will soon return to the table with an artificial grin and the query "Are you guys ready to order?" My mother, who is over seventy and a mother of four, is categorically not "you guys," but waiters invariably seem to think that she would *like* to be. Not that she complains—she's a good sport, and is usually too worried that the kitchen will slip a rack of ribs into her vegetarian pasta to trouble with forms of address—but it irks me, her youngest and long-disrespectful son. The fact that my wife and I are also "you guys" is a minor matter in comparison. The gender attribution is less of an issue here than its forced casualness. The word "guy," after all, is slang. Its nearest equivalent in French, and surely its semantic progenitor, is *gars.* "Hi guys," becomes *Salut les gars.* One need only imagine a self-respecting French waiter addressing an elderly couple as *les gars* to know how far from that standard we Americans have devolved. Call me retro, but call my mother ma'am.

If I thought it through, at the corner of Balzac and Friedland, I would conclude that I am nervous because I am foreign, because I am not accustomed to eating this way, and because I suspect that there are things one absolutely does not say or do in the dining room of this restaurant that we, or I, will say or do. I dread the near-certainty that common courtesy and good manners will not suffice. Something will slip, some gaffe, made all the worse because it will be committed in ignorance, and with the best of intentions. We will break a cardinal law of French etiquette, something more heinous, perhaps, than licking our fingers and wiping our chins with the tablecloth, and we will do it with gravity and politesse. We both know that it is acceptable and expected in France to "mop"—to clean the remaining sauce from one's plate with a slice of baguette, an act of barbarism at self-respecting tables of the United States. For reasons that remain unclear—my Scotch-Canadian grandmother, perhaps—I was raised to eat in the continental fashion, wherein it is permissible to spear a morsel with the fork in the left hand, tines down, and raise the bite directly to the mouth—another faux pas, generally speaking, *en Amérique*. And we know that one uses the silverware from the outside in as the meal progresses. But otherwise we're on our own. The problem with etiquette is that it is a language, like Urdu; it is not intuitive, but learned.

On the one hand, I think, if I forget myself and smell the cork, so be it. Such a thing is never done by people who actually know wines, because the odor of the cork reveals precisely nothing. Or, rather, it reveals one's ignorance, and one's desire to be admired as worldly. The fact that one is surrounded by men who smell their corks at overpriced business lunches in mediocre restaurants does not lend credence to the act. In any case, there should be no reason, really, that one should be expected to do anything more than behave according to the laws of natural courtesy, especially if one is having a meal for the price of a used car.

Whereas Erin's anxiety may be natural, mine is more puzzling on the face of it, for I have been apprenticing at Taillevent off and on over the last three months. With the permission of owner Jean-Claude Vrinat and his two chefs, I have become a kind of reporter-apprentice and ambulatory traffic cone in the kitchens. When I am not harrying the chefs with questions, snacking on petits-fours in the pastry kitchen, or wolfing down small offerings in the *cuisine*, I am doing some small task half as well, and twice as slowly, as the greenest young cook in the house. I remove shards of shell from trays of crabmeat, press rings of dough into baking tins smaller than shot glasses, pass a torch over *Crèmes brûlées à la Bergamote*, cut rose petals from sheets of white chocolate.

Having worked, years before, as a prep cook, waiter, and bartender in a number of American restaurants, I had long harbored an interest in seeing a French kitchen at work. This interest was more personal than professional: my restaurant days were probably over, but I wanted to know more about what professional cooks thought and felt about food. I was somewhat less interested in technique than in attitude, approach. I wondered, for example, how a professional chef might prepare a meal for a loved one, and how his or her professional experience might aid or hinder it. Does increased technical knowledge expand one's awareness and appreciation of fundamental human experience, or does it create a gap, an alienating objectivity? It is an age-old question, and the answer goes both ways. As a writer by trade, with much to learn, I find it difficult to suppress the trained impulse to craft language, however casual the written form. Because of this, I have found that experience as a writer both helps and interferes with my ability to be simple and direct.

As a boy of eighteen in Washington, D.C., I often drove down to the Vietnam Veterans Memorial late at night. I would read the notes to dead soldiers, short or long letters from wives and sisters and mothers and grown sons, as often as not written at something like the sixth-grade level. The simplest and quietest, the most everyday, were always the truest and most heartbreaking. I knew even then that no amount of craft could improve them.

So I was and remain unsure about the value of so-called expertise when it comes to things that matter more than art or engineering. As for food, I was only just beginning to understand the significance of meals in a family and among friends. Our first child, a daughter, had been born not three years before this period in France. In the first days home from the hospital my wife, who had been through an arduous labor, was pale and weak from loss of blood and spent much of her time in bed. The first morning home I had no appetite at all, too wired and apprehensive and ecstatic as I was, but my wife was ravenous. I hurried downstairs in the early morning and made a six-egg omelet splitting with avocado and melted jack cheese and tomatoes, with sheaves of toast and half a grapefruit besides. I poured her a wineglass full of whole milk—something she never ordinarily drinks. When I carried it up to her, I sat on the edge of a chair near the bed and watched her eat while the baby slept curled up against her hip. Without abandoning her manners, she ate like an animal that has been near death and is recovering. I could not look away; it was as if I could see the lost blood returning to her veins, spun from the cells of the meal, the forces of regeneration aglow in the room. In that period of half an hour, from the moment I cracked the first egg into the bowl until she had eaten the very last of it, to the crumb, and sagged back, sated, into the pillows, I understood food and what it means to cook in a way I never have before or since.

Food is love, I used to joke—embittered by my mother's small servings at the dinner table—and I'm hungry. Why my mother served so little pasta, for example, rather than the indecorous mounds we might consume, remains a mystery. The mere presence of food in the fridge always seemed to distress her, and when one of us returned from a run to the market with two bags of groceries, she would invariably remark, "Goodness, we'll have enough food for a month!"

In defiance of her inclinations, my mother is still able to produce a superb lasagna, the best pasta puttanesca I've ever had, and an excellent roast chicken, among other things. Repressed may it be, an aptitude for cooking lurks within her. It has been telling to note how this played out in my two sisters. One, dismayed by my mother's approach to homemaking, embraced the hearth and stove with a vengeance. The other has maintained the belief, staunchly held and widely publicized, that she cannot cook an egg, despite countless other creative talents.

When I was a boy, my father rarely cooked. But when he and I drove north to the Catskills to visit his mother, he would cook dinner for the three of us. The meal was invariably a steak and a baked potato and green beans or carrots steamed and sautéed in butter. It was always tasty and serviceable, and in every way a mysterious reflection of the man. My father was eternally on edge in that grand house—his mother was difficult. But I always had the sense, as we ate his meals to the sound of silverware in the dim light at that long table, that I was learning something about my father that could not otherwise be learned or put to words. More recently, now retired, my father has developed a real enthusiasm for cooking. He writes down recipes at dinner parties. He does most of the cooking for the two of them, and when my parents last visited he prepared an enormous and delicious eggplant casserole with Gruyère and tomatoes and parsley and sautéed onions, and it was a joy to see how much fun he had putting it all together.

My first real exposure to France and the French attitude toward food came at nineteen, when I saved up some money and spent six months traveling through Europe. I slept out under bushes in Paris and on the floors of apartments, and had no funds for anything as extravagant as a meal at a starred restaurant, but I spent plenty of time around tables of one kind or another, in small apartments and in bistros, and I soon understood how differently the French perceived meals. My clearest memory of this distinction involves a meal in no way particularly French. Soon after my arrival in Paris, an American friend and I were invited to a small dinner party in a tiny apartment in the Sixth Arrondissement, a mix of ex-pats and Parisians in their twenties and thirties. We all helped cook. The dish was a very simple pasta with a red sauce, and there was a *salade verte,* and bottles of inexpensive Côtes du Rhône, and some very good cheeses at the end. Everyone smoked more or less incessantly, and the conversation, to my ear, could not have been improved. There was some kind of festival in the quarter, for we leaned out of the windows and watched people milling cheerfully past.

As I would soon discover, it was just like nearly any other simple dinner party in Paris. As a newcomer, I was transfixed. It was the pace, mostly, and the manner of the French. They listened more closely. They watched you when you spoke. They were both intent and languid. They did not seem, as Americans so often do, even in times of leisure, hurried or distracted. When they ate, they appeared to taste and savor carefully, but without fanfare. It was as if they had been raised to pay attention in a way we had forgotten, or discarded as impractical. One of the women at the party later drove me to Montmartre, on a pale-grey November after-noon, when the Place du Tertre was cold and aban-doned and lovely. Where are we? I asked her, amazed. What village is this? It's still Paris, she said, it's Mont-martre. She had the habit of using her hands to see. She would run her hands over trees, stones, iron bars. "Are you angry?" she would often ask me in English, mean-ing hungry, and I would say, Yes, I am angry, let's eat.

I appeared at Taillevent largely by chance. Months before, I had seen a series of compelling interviews with French chefs; two of the most interesting, to my mind, were pastry chef Gilles Bajolle and *chef de cui-sine* Philippe Legendre. Without knowing where they worked, I tracked down Bajolle in Paris in April of 1999. Both he and Legendre, I discovered, worked at Taillevent. Unsurprisingly, given their place of employ, both were leaders in the field, each widely considered to be among a handful of the finest chefs in the world. I met first with Bajolle, and then Legendre, and arranged to do an informal, open-ended *stage,* or apprentice-ship, at the restaurant. Whereas the formal apprentices work day after day for long hours, to their benefit, I have moved in and out of the apprentice role. One morning, I might work as an apprentice in the pastry kitchen; after lunch, I might exchange my white jacket, kerchief, and apron for a pen, and spend the afternoon in the *cuisine* taking notes. The following day, these roles might reverse. All in all, I have spent somewhat more time in the pastry department than the main kitchen. In the *laboratoire*, as the pastry kitchen is known, the climate is more amicable, the chef more conversant, and the fresh, homemade ice cream nearer at hand.

And yet I have had little or no contact with the servers, and when I reserved our table some days before, I did not alert the host that I was the same fellow apprenticing in the kitchen. He did not appear to recognize my name, fortunately, and I decided against notifying the owner or the chefs that I would be coming to eat. Not out of any desire for secrecy, but to avoid, as much as possible, the risk of special treatment. I wanted to come as an ordinary guest, with my wife, and eat dinner. For that reason, I suppose, I feel nearly as much uncertainty and apprehension, as we sit in the car and watch the clock tick, as I might were this another place entirely. In much the same way, I imagine, that an inexperienced actor might be struck with anxiety when going out onstage for the first time, despite weeks of working as a stagehand in the same theater.

After ten minutes of alternating silence and scraps of conversation so innocuous and forced that neither of us will be able to recall a word of it by the time we reach the opposing curb, we climb out of the car, brush the automotive wrinkles out of our clothing, and set off, arm in arm, toward our fate.

"You look wonderful," I say as we mount the sidewalk and start down the rue Lamennais. My wife doesn't believe me. She is feeling self-conscious about her choice of dress, a pale-blue and subtly floral affair, elegantly cut but almost certainly, she realizes, too casual in context. I approved it, badgering her to get out the door, but that's no excuse. Perfect for an August wedding, but dinner, in Paris, at Taillevent? And these sandals. This purse! She wants to climb into my hip pocket and vanish.

I had little choice. My best black suit, an Italian tie. For all I know, I look like an undertaker on the dole.

Even had our aging sedan been more presentable—and at Taillevent, creased bumper or no, how could it possibly be?—I would never have driven to the door. I abhor valet service, and will go to any lengths to avoid it. For one thing, I dislike the invariable manner of valets. I have stood near the entrance of hotels and restaurants, waiting for a cab or an appointment, and watched valets park and retrieve cars. I never like what I see. They slouch and smoke around the valet booth like drug dealers, and when they get a fare they move too fast, snapping with their hands at the proffered keys (and later, folded bills) like pit bulls, without a gracious word. Then they throw themselves behind the wheel with that loose-limbed, hip-hop propriety, as if these were *their wheels*, presuming instant familiarity with the vehicle's functions, slamming the door with a shudder, and bolting from a standing start to squeal off into their suspiciously unseen parking lots. The few times I have been forced by circumstance to accept valet service, I have found it almost nauseating, as if I were being carjacked. None of which, of course, would I vocally admit. Such sentiments, I know, are profoundly neurotic and misanthropic. They run counter to what I might vaguely (and with only mild derision) define as my "deeper values." And they surprise me, too, since I have worked, in younger incarnations, on construction crews. Between the ages of eighteen and twenty-two, among other jobs, I poured concrete, built decks, and erected fences. I also guarded beaches, tended bar, and waited tables, and might well have worked as a valet, had the opportunity presented itself, without undue discomfort. I once read that, whatever a man may become in later life, if he has ever worked construction, on a crew, he will never feel that prim, ineffectual self-consciousness that Men in Suits may feel as they walk stiff-legged past a construction site. For some time I took comfort in that assertion, and found it true. I would pass construction sites with interest, occasionally pausing to watch the machines and, more rarely, chat with workers on break; we would end up trading stories—dramatic falls and other injuries, building-inspector nightmares, broken gas lines.

But now, little more than a decade after my last manual job and five years into a happy marriage, I am not so sure. In boots and jeans, perhaps, I can still connect with my inner laborer. But put me in a suit and a wool coat on the corner of Lexington and 34th, hurrying to an editorial appointment, and make me wait for a light beside a road crew, close enough to taste the smoke of their menthol cigarettes, my gaze fixed on the distant crossing light, and I too will burn with that class shame. And when I cross, finally, liberated by the changing light, I will raise my free hand, palm upward, and study it briefly—its mate burdened by a briefcase—this hand, once callused, hatched with cuts, and think how soft, how *bookish* these hands have become.

We arrive at Taillevent, on foot, at precisely 8:30 p.m. There is no one in sight on the sidewalk in either direction. The entrance to the restaurant is so understated that one could quite easily drive past, by day or night, without remarking it. Above the doorway at 15, rue Lamennais is a trim metal awning, painted forest green, with stenciled gold letters,

TAILLEVENT

The awning is something you might expect to find above a stone portal at Wimbledon. No sooner do we appear in the faint lamplight beneath the awning than the door glides silently open, like a protective wing of darkened glass. I take my wife by the elbow. And we step through.

L'Apéritif

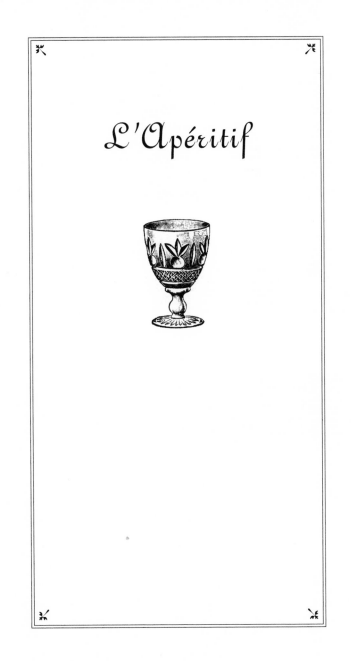

We are met by a tall, broad-shouldered *maître d'hôtel* in a black suit and bow tie. He greets us with a half-bow, a sweeping gesture of the left arm, and a smile so warm and apparently sincere that we wonder if we've come to the right place. In sheer elasticity and expressive range, it is a face that Marcel Marceau could envy. From the mound in Yankee Stadium, this man's smile would reach the upper decks.

Green umbrellas stand in racks on either side of the vestibule. Two paintings hang from mirrored walls: A medieval town and harbor of the Low Countries faces a religious procession in a generic countryside, led by figures clad in white and accompanied by horsemen. A small white church, their destination, stands at the peak of a hill.

The *maître d'* makes a mark beside our name on a small pad and draws us through the vestibule into the entry hall with a stride so liquid as to be indistinguishable from levitation. We follow him into the hall as he floats on, a step and a half ahead of us, his torso and head turning slightly now and then in our direction, his back straight, his left arm extended as if to indicate and clear the way, his right held toward us, as if to enclose us and protect our flank—a noble posture, respectful yet unobsequious. It is that rarest of performances that one suspects could not be perceptibly improved. Other figures in black jackets appear as if from all directions. We have the impression of being instantaneously and comfortably surrounded by silent attendants. The light in the entry hall is golden and subdued, dreamlike in comparison with the still, stony darkness of the rue Lamennais.

A woman emerges from the doorway of a brightly lit coatroom, and takes a step toward us as we approach. She stops, stands politely, smiles a decorous and receptive smile, a smile that gives the impression that she is not only pleased to see us, but subtly *basking* in our mere proximity. It is the kind of smile that we, more accustomed to the wry detachment of the Parisian café-and-bistro waiter, might believe to be reserved for royalty, shipping magnates, and, say, Emmanuelle Béart on the arm of Daniel Auteuil. It is the kind of smile that the finest professionals in the service industry all possess in variation, a smile that succeeds, miraculously, because it is on some level genuine.

Behind the coat checker, hidden from view, is the *vestiaire* itself, with facing racks of wooden hangers and cubbies stocked with stain remover, talcum powder, and paper handkerchiefs. A tray of scissors, needles, and other domestic hardware stands on one shelf. To preserve the dignity and comfort of her guests in the face of any conceivable culinary or digestive mishap, Madame du Vestiaire is equipped, one suspects, to perform anything from a quick buff of a gravy-spattered wing-tip to an emergency appendectomy.

L'Apéritif

I wonder if she has a fire extinguisher handy, for I once saw someone in a restaurant set on fire. A waiter, jostled by another guest, bobbled and then spilled a bowl of flaming pudding on the head and bare neck of a woman at a neighboring table in suburban New York, circa 1974. Already delighted and mystified by the blue blaze (at eight, I had never seen a dessert, indoors, on fire), I observed it all. The waiter's approach, the guest's rise, the bump, the lurching tray, the bowl as it skidded down the circular rail to wobble and then—oh yes!—to fall. The pudding burned in her hair like Sterno fuel, a cheerful flame, as she leapt from her seat. I believe I cheered. The alcohol in the pudding winked out fast enough to avoid injury, but her hair and the pudding fared poorly.

And though I have never witnessed an actual administration of the Heimlich maneuver, I recall the true story of the man who, dared by a friend, attempted to swallow an entire steak—a half-pound slab of elastic bovine muscle—unchewed and in one gulp. No amount of friendly violence would budge the resulting obstruction, and I believe he was buried with the steak *in situ*. A piscivorous variation of this occurred more recently on a fishing dory. A drunken youth of questionable judgment offered to swallow a whole live trout for five dollars. He met with the same end—his partner claimed he couldn't get a decent grip on the trout's slick tail. What a scene! I'm sure the trout's captured colleagues, observing from a pail, took dark pleasure in the sight of an angler thrashing, expiring for want of air in the bottom of his own boat.

More harmlessly, I have seen quite a number of diners dampened. Most such incidents were resolved amicably, but one stands out in memory. The year following high school, determined at the time to avoid higher education, I took a job waiting tables at a Georgetown restaurant. One evening, a waiter spilled a glass of water on the shirt of an elegantly dressed dinner guest. The victim leapt to his feet and all but accused the server of battery. He demanded the manager, a stocky Dartmouth graduate, who quickly appeared. Despite redundant apologies and the assurance that the restaurant would pay his dry-cleaning bill, the customer became increasingly irate. All conversation in the restaurant ceased. Sir, it was only *water,* the manager finally said with exasperation. The man made some angry retort, and the manager lost his composure. "I'm melllltinggggggg," he shrieked in falsetto, and executed a full-blown pantomime of the Wicked Witch of the West, doused in water and dissolving into smoke. From the theatrical point of view, it was as brilliant as it was unexpected. A deathly silence followed. All of us—staff, other guests, the victim, and his mortified companion—were dumbstruck. And yet it put an end to the dispute. The shock seemed to return the man to his senses. He sat down with perfect dignity and ate his dinner. I believe the manager sent him a bottle of wine.

In Taillevent's carpeted entry hall, the walls are painted cream. Small upholstered benches stand against the walls. To the left are wood-paneled washrooms, momentarily in shadow. Motion-sensitive, their lights do not wink on abruptly but *rise* upon the entrance of a guest. Cast bronze dolphins spout water into marble sinks.

Facing the *vestiaire*, an antique metal clock, supported by a dancing cherub, stands on a table beside a glass ashtray that by appearances has never known the effrontery of a cigarette. Continuing through open double doors, we pass a bar of polished marble under glass. A lone bartender is pouring champagne. Behind him hangs an eighteenth-century Beauvais tapestry of two large haughty-looking birds of unknown species— possibly albino peacocks—courting in a wooded glade. In the tapestry's middle distance, beneath the boughs of the trees, lie the arches of an ancient aqueduct.

As we round the corner and enter the dining room, all of this conspires to create, before we have even been seated, a mildly altered state of consciousness. It is the sense, most of all, of being almost supernaturally welcomed and cared for. To the unaccustomed, as with any performance art, such a restaurant is far enough outside the realm of the ordinary that it seems to operate under enchantment.

Behind a closed door at the end of the hall, beyond the bar, is the central control room, a small office occupied by a desk, a human being, and what appear to be enough computers, monitors, printers, and other terminals to operate a nuclear submarine. We do not see this cold and imposing chamber, but it is there, the twenty-first-century brain of a nineteenth-century mansion.

The private home that is now Taillevent was built in

1852—the first year of the Second Empire—by the Duc de Morny, the Emperor's half-brother and minister of the interior. Elsewhere in that year, Elisha Graves Otis invented the modern elevator in Yonkers, New York, and the thirty-three-year-old Ivan Turgenev published *A Sportsman's Sketches*. For many years, the mansion housed the Embassy of Paraguay. Restaurateur André Vrinat founded Taillevent in 1946, near the Place Saint-Georges. The restaurant thrived, receiving its first Michelin star in 1948. In 1950, Vrinat moved his operation to its present address on the rue Lamennais, a few minutes' walk from the Champs-Élysées, in the Eighth Arrondissement. Michelin awarded Vrinat's restaurant, now a landmark, its second star in 1956. André Vrinat was joined by his son Jean-Claude, a graduate of the Haute École Commerciale, the Harvard Business School of France, in 1962. They earned their third and final star in 1973.

Taillevent was the alias of Guillaume Tirel, a notoriously overweight and talented fourteenth-century French chef who spent most of his career cooking for kings. Starting out as a kitchen boy for Jeanne d'Évreux, Taillevent went on to cook for Philippe de Valois, the Duke of Normandy, Charles V, and Charles VI. At the request of Charles V, Taillevent compiled the first known cookbook in 1379, a treatise on the preparation of meats and other dishes entitled *Le Viandier*. The esteemed chef, whose crest bears three stockpots surrounded by six roses, died in 1395 at the age of eighty-five, and now lies buried west of Paris. *Le Viandier* is still in print; collectors are directed to La Librairie des Gourmets, a culinary bookshop on the rue Monge. Consider renting a *camionnette* for this outing: the shop is a deathtrap for Francophonic bibliophiles with even a passing interest in food. At last sight, La Librairie had limited-edition copies of Taillevent's opus, stout as Latin dictionaries, on a high shelf behind the cashier.

The true restaurant is a signature device of civilization, a commercial formalization of what might be our species' oldest form of social kindness (after the permitted ravishing), hospitality. As soon as we formed alliances beyond the limits of blood kin, we began to have friends over for dinner. Neanderthals surely entertained. From such times forward, to share a meal would evoke one of our most potent and enduring cultural laws, akin to the handshake as a seal of faith: do not betray those with whom you have broken bread. Camus's short story "L'Hôte" (which translates as both "Host" and "Guest") is a study of this principle. A French schoolteacher in Algeria is directed by local authorities to accompany a North African murderer to prison and certain execution. The teacher feeds and shelters his prisoner before starting out. Having been the man's host, the Frenchman finds he cannot turn him in, and sets him free. In kind, because he was fed and sheltered by the Frenchman, the North African surrenders himself to the authorities and certain death to prevent incriminating his host.

The *maître d'* leads us through the bipartite dining room on the ground floor, past the foot of a curving, carpeted marble staircase equipped with a gilded wrought-iron banister. Passing French and Flemish oils of the seventeenth and eighteenth centuries, and niches shelved with silver, bronze, and ceramic objets d'art, we continue through a doorway flanked by compound Ionic columns, and arrive at our table. Another *maître d'*, a captain, draws the table out and away from a banquette with a crisp, abbreviated bow. This is my wife's first disappointment. We will be sitting side by side, on what is for all intents and purposes a bench, and though she knows that I might actually favor such an arrangement—I have often remarked that I find it easier to talk in the car, sharing the same view, than face-to-face—she decidedly does not. She prefers, and unconsciously expected, the enclosed, intimate setting of a corner table or a booth for two. For one, she likes to look at the person to whom she's talking without getting a stiff neck. Sitting side by side will also make her feel exposed, on display. Her natural position will direct her attention outward, into a foreign space occupied by others, instead of inward, toward her mate. This will certainly diminish, if not seriously disrupt, the evening's expectedly romantic aspect. Some intimate dinner for two, she thinks, surprised by her own peevishness. Given the setting, and the silken orchestration of our entrance, it hardly seems appropriate to ask if there is another, more private table available. She also knows that I would be appalled by such a complaint, however delicately expressed. And that, though I might silently endure its outcome, the meal would commence under a gloom that would never entirely dissipate. As it happens, the eight other tables in our section are occupied, including another banquette, from whose vantage an elderly French couple gazes curiously out across the room like a pair of barn owls, nibbling their appetizers in silence. So Erin says nothing, broadens her smile for the second *maître d'*, and slips into her seat behind the table.

In point of fact, I am also mildly dismayed by the arrangement, but, given the unjustifiable financial investment, and how impressed I have been by the welcome, I push my disappointment vigorously from my mind. I attempt to convince myself that in some way the bench must actually be superior to the commonplace vis-à-vis position. There is something potentially exotic, I suspect, about the single banquette for two. I determine to ask a knowledgeable friend of mine about the distinction, about the origin and benefits of this sidelong arrangement, and sit down.

I also feel a measure of relief—I will not be forced to face my wife directly during the meal. I have always found her intimidating head-on in a restaurant. In such a setting, stiffened by what I perceive to be her intense romantic expectation, I have a hard time meeting her eye until the second or third glass of wine. She also regards me with particular intensity at restaurants, as if she is attempting to read my cluttered mind. In fact, she is probably trying to escape from the inevitable self-consciousness of public dining, and into the psychic wind tunnel of marital eye contact.

We are seated at 8:32—two minutes after crossing the threshold—and one minute later the captain sets a silver tray of gougères before us. A three-star cheese puff of flour, egg, and Gruyère, the gougère has been served as the lead *amuse-bouche* (literally, amuse-mouth) since 1974. Mr. Vrinat decided upon them in part because they are dry to the touch: this prevents the transmission of grease from the diners' fingers to the immaculate menus to come. The gougères are mild, classic, and unpretentious, in complexity a step above popcorn. They are tasty enough, but dazzle neither eye nor tongue, an effect that has hardly been lost on Vrinat, *chef de cuisine* Philippe Legendre, or *chef de patisserie* Gilles Bajolle—the three men most closely involved with Taillevent's menu. I later inquired of Bajolle why they find the humble gougère to be the perfect introduction to what may be the world's finest cooking. "If you serve something more complex as an *amuse-bouche*," he said, "it undermines the taste of the apéritif."

In French, the captain asks if we would like a drink, compliments of the house, before dinner. Determined to be festive, I order a dry Kir Royale. Erin rarely drinks, although she loves the scent of ale decanted into a glass, and will drink a glass of Bordeaux, when I'm pouring, to be companionable. But she has a more sensitive palate, and finds many wines that I like undrinkable. At the moment she wants nothing more than a faintly sweet, decidedly nonalcoholic drink—but she knows she must drink *something* alcoholic, right now, or make me unhappy. She defers to the captain, who suggests, in a voice just shy of insistence, a *cocktail maison*. "You'll have to help me drink it," she whispers, leaning close and squeezing my hand invisibly as the captain withdraws to collect our drinks, and for a moment we're both legitimately pleased by the banquette.

The apéritifs are set down at 8:36. The *cocktail maison*, served in a glass goblet over ice, is red and punchy and in alcohol content very nearly flammable. Erin takes one sip and restrains herself, puckering her lips ever so slightly and blowing through them, as if to clear the vapor from her mouth. At home, when she nicks a sip of my Scotch, lured by its smell, she wrinkles her nose dramatically, ponies her head violently from side to side, thrusts out her tongue, coughs, and makes a panting, waggling sound of pain and disgust. I find this mannerism charming. She would certainly make the same facial gesture here—it tastes like cherry gasoline, chemical and toxic—but she confines it to the pucker, glances at the nearest servers, who appear to be both ubiquitous and invisible, to see if her displeasure was observed, encounters no crestfallen gaze, sets down the goblet, and slowly pushes it four inches across the tablecloth in my direction. "Wow," she says under her breath. The Kir Royale is not quite as dry as I had hoped— they never are; not even, I discover, at Taillevent—but it is delicious all the same.

As we finish off the last of the gougères, I steadily drain Erin's cocktail at her behest. For once she was not exaggerating: the *cocktail maison* is about as potent as a punch can be without evaporating out of the glass. A mixture of raspberry pulp, *crème de framboise*, Grand Marnier, and champagne, it manages to go down like 151-proof rum over crushed fruit. Nonetheless, it is tasty after a fashion, and I welcome its anesthetic wallop.

At 8:40, Jean-Claude Vrinat arrives at our table. It is impossible to determine if he is surprised to see me, or if he had read the guest list earlier and recalled the name. He seems to remember me now—if only vaguely, for I have had as yet no real contact with him, aside from an introductory handshake and an occasional word of greeting in the corridors. To his credit, he seems entirely neutral to the presence of an American reporter in his kitchens. This evening, he has been circulating quietly throughout the dining room, shaking the odd hand, engaging in what appears to be light conversation punctuated with wise smiles and self-deprecatory nods. Now he welcomes us, and hands us our menus with the faintest bow.

La Carte

Minestrone d'Artichauts Poivrade au Pistou, it begins, at the top of a column of *entrées,* or first courses. In France, of course, the *entrée,* or "entry" into the meal, is not a main dish, or *plat,* but an appetizer. How this became confused in translation into English is beyond me, but I'm sure there is the willful mischief of a seventeenth-century French diplomat to blame. The folded rectangular menus are large and elegant, printed on stiff, cream-colored paper. When closed, they are more than a foot and a half tall by a foot wide. On the front page, appetizers, fish, and meat and game are separated by engravings. The wine list occupies two facing pages within.

I know immediately that I did not come to Taillevent for anything resembling minestrone, however sublime or unorthodox, and jump ahead with mild irritation. As much as the thought of artichokes *à la poivrade* (typically a kind of pepper vinaigrette) coupled with the garlic and basil normally associated with *pistou,* a Provençale soup, might appeal to me, I feel surprised, even ambushed, by the word "minestrone" in a restaurant of this stature, in France. Although I may not have known it, the word "minestrone," or the host of images it conjured, was one of the innumerable things I hoped to evade in moving to Europe. Not that my associations

with the soup were in any overt way identifiably negative: stacks of blue cans on the shelves of the Grand
Union in a suburban New York town, unprepossessing
Italian restaurants, bowls of my mother's minestrone on
our dinner table (and with the bowls come the woven
blue and slightly rumpled cotton place mats, the small,
chipped crystal bowls of salt and pepper, each furnished
with a tarnished silver spoon no more substantial than a
sparrow's rib, the silver napkin rings engraved with the
initials of long-dead relatives, and the floating, ambient
cat hair that somehow made its way into every dish
served in that house).

When I recovered our car in Le Havre, on a drizzling
January day six months before, having shipped it from
the end of a New Jersey pier, and pulled finally onto
the highway toward our rented apartment off the rue
Lepic in Paris, I felt an immeasurable sense of lightness and renewal. Above all, I felt a sense of possibility
more profound than any I had had since my early
twenties—since the largely illusory promise of dawn-
ing adulthood. Illusory because, apart from attractive
and vivacious company, nothing comes of youth and
ambition without the sustained and patient effort that
ambitious youth too often finds tedious. I had lived in
France sporadically over the past decade, a year here, a
year and a half there, each time returning to the States
for ostensibly practical reasons—to finish my degree
in the first case, and later to marry on family ground.
But this move to Europe was potentially permanent. I
shipped nearly everything we owned as an anchor, a

dead weight to discourage retreat. Since the appearance of our daughter, two at the time of our move, this anchor had gained appreciably in mass. Let's start with a few years, I said to my wife, and then we'll see. I hoped she would agree to stay indefinitely. What *of* the smoke screens in the restaurants, the drifts of dog excrement, the bureaucrats, and the bleak, endless industrial winters? This is *France.* As I upshifted and changed lanes, gaining speed, scanning the highway— French pavings, French road signs, French license plates on French cars—a soaring buoyancy rushed through me. I felt like shouting, and did: I whooped in the car. Yes! I bellowed. Yes! I pounded the steering wheel, crushed it in my grip, pounded it again, and flew on. And though I did not at the time think in any such specifics, I knew that the minestrone, and the cat hair, and the napkin rings of dead and faceless relatives (I myself would be a dead and faceless relative soon enough, as I well knew) hadn't made it onto the boat.

Or so it first appeared. As I would ordinarily be quick to acknowledge, each of us is a Trojan Horse, packed with the Greeks of our pasts. But, for a moment, for a few exquisite months, I thought I had actually managed to cut loose and had left Troy to burn.

In any case, I did not come to Taillevent for a bowl of minestrone. I read on.

Royale de Champignons à l'Aigre-Doux
Crème de Cresson au Caviar Sevruga
Asperges vertes poêlées au Jus de Truffes

It goes without saying that we will try the asparagus. I believe there is no vegetable—indeed, no edible object of any kingdom—which rivals the asparagus properly cooked. When singing the praises of that green shoot, or defending its virtue against attacks of indifference, I might even be mistaken as a foodie. I owe this largely to my college adviser, an eclectic savant, misanthrope, and self-exiled inhabitant of the seventeenth century, who, while disabusing me of my misconceptions surrounding Virginia Woolf, Franz Schubert, and the student films of Roman Polanski over dinner, introduced me to asparagus properly steamed, and to a simple dipping sauce of mayonnaise, Dijon mustard, and dill. My debt for this recipe shall never fully be repaid. The list continues:

Escargots braisés, Sauce Poulette
Ballotine de Foie gras de Canard
Mousseline d'Oeufs aux Morilles et aux Asperges
Raviolis de Fromage de Chèvre à l'Armoricaine
Cannellonis de Tourteau, Sauce Ravigote
Boudin de Homard à la Nage

The main courses follow. The fish:

Daurade à la Tomate et au Basilic
Rougets en Filets aux Anchois et au Fenouil
Bar de Ligne au gros Sel
Sole en Filets au Cresson de Fontaine, Sauce
    Marinière
Darne de Turbot rôtie au Beurre fumé

La Carte

Fricassée de Langoustines en Cassolette
Homard poêlé aux Châtaignes

Followed by the meat and game:

Pigeon rôti en Bécasse
Poulette de Bresse en Cocotte lutée (2 personnes)
Canette de Challans au Miel et au Citron
        (2 personnes)
Andouillette de Pied de Porc aux Truffes
Foie de Canard poêlé au Poivre torréfié
Selle d'Agneau farcie au Jus de Truffes
        (2 personnes)
Côte de Veau fermier à l'Oseille
Escalope de Ris de Veau aux Morilles
Cœur de Filet de Bœuf en Pissaladière
Côte de Bœuf grillée aux trois Sauces (2 personnes)

As we read the menu, unhurried, each of us is lost in a succession of oral fantasies engendered, one after another, by the barrage of culinary flavors, aspects, and methods. I move down the list, weighing choices, while saliva gradually pools in the well beneath my tongue. Closely read, a good menu is an onslaught, and, like the flickering response to an equivalent string of bodily terms—lips, breasts, thighs, feet—each word or phrase on the menu, particularly something like "sautéed in truffle juice," or "roasted in smoked butter," thumps and shudders like a depth charge in the animal mind. *Beurre, crème, fenouil, basilic, sauce, jus, poêlée.* The impact of this verbal suggestion is heightened by contextual anticipation (I *know* we will be eating in this quarter-hour), like erotic innuendo in a taxi home. The impact of such language can attain an excruciating pitch if reflected upon in times of forced abstinence.

In August of 1982, before my junior year in high school, a friend and I took a month-long course in mountaineering and wilderness survival through the National Outdoor Leadership School in Lander, Wyoming. At month's end, fit as Olympians but wraithlike, we hiked out of Wyoming's Wind River Range to the road head in small groups, a four- or five-day trek, fasting. The fast was a crowning indignity; we had survived the month on little more than dried fruit, bulgur, and Grape-Nuts. Our external-frame packs weighed more than seventy pounds, including climbing equipment, camping gear, and emergency rations, and we were hiking as much as thirteen miles a day, route-finding with map and compass through wilderness. The hollow pain in our bellies seemed to peak and subside on the second day, but by the last night, camped under a tarp in sight of the pickup zone, we were delirious, semihallucinatory, and the pain returned. As we had come down out of the mountains, into the arid foothills of Wyoming in late August, many of the springs on the map had proved dry. Despite conservation, we ran out of water near the middle of the last day, and added dehydration to our discomforts. Unable to sleep, we spent most of that last night writing lists of all the sweet and savory things we would consume, and in what order, on our return to civilization. One of us would call out an entry; after a silent moment of absorption would rise a chorus of oaths and moans.

"Philly cheese steak, covered in onions . . ."

"Don't say it."

"A big oily sausage-and-pepperoni pizza . . ."

"Ohhh, you bastard."

"A Double Whopper," rasped a parched voice in the darkness, "with bacon and cheese, large fries, and a Coke." The company groaned like dogs.

Other entries on my personal list of nearly a hundred items included Key lime pie, lobster rolls, jelly doughnuts, and Buffalo wings. Red meat and pizza reappeared in countless forms. Greasy substances, high in fat and protein, were the staples on everybody's list, the T & A of our culinary pornography. Around three in the morning, overcome with desperation, I ate a few inches of toothpaste and gagged.

Soon after dawn, when the bus appeared in the distance, throwing up a rooster tail of dust, we ran down to the road like liberated POWs, braying for food and water. They gave us plastic bowls of cornflakes immediately, with sliced banana and skim milk — nothing too complex for our withered viscera. The sweet and milky taste was wondrous, but the *sensation* of something substantial—something that could be chewed and consumed—was so intense as to seem unprecedented, as if we had never before eaten solid food. Later, we learned that the other groups had broken into their emergency rations in the first two days. How we scorned them.

On our return to Lander, disregarding our instructors' warnings, we ate as much meat, fat, and candy as we could get our hands on. In a rural, Western American town, this amounted to a good deal. Alone and with others, I systematically combed the grid of downtown Lander, hitting every fast-food place and convenience store in my path. I scratched items, one after another, from my list. Double cheeseburgers, chocolate bars, steak sandwiches, vats of soda and lemonade, huge, loaded pizzas wolfed down alone in a corner booth.

The morning after our return, the very instant I awakened in our hotel room, I sprang out of bed with the intention of cleaning out the adjacent doughnut shop. I took one half-conscious bound down the staircase, missed the fifth step I had aimed for, and tumbled end over end to the next landing. Thirty seconds later, rubbing my elbows, I stood before the shop's glass cabinet, peering in. Glazed doughnuts, powdered doughnuts, chocolate doughnuts, cinnamon doughnuts, jelly doughnuts, old-fashioneds, crullers, twists, éclairs. Row upon row, illuminated, under glass.

This three-day orgy destroyed my digestion for months, and at the time I could feel it happening—all that heavy protein backing up in my intestines like wet sand. But I couldn't stop; the imperative to eat was too strong.

I have never sat down to a meal in quite the same way since, and for the first seven or eight years the sense memory and the fear of that hunger stayed near

me. More often than I would have expected, as I set into
something as simple as a cheese sandwich, I would
remember that hunger—it would rush me like violence
relived—and I would eat the sandwich like a dying
man.

At Taillevent, our appetites enflamed, Erin and I
consult conspiratorially, in low tones. The importance
of this moment is often overlooked. If the apéritif
marks its nativity, pondering the menu is a meal's
youth. Like that period in one's early life when one is
regaled with unrealized choices, the short span of minutes just prior to declaring your order must be properly
observed and appreciated. Then, and only then, everything on the menu is yours.

With the understanding that we can hardly err, we
tentatively decide to split a bowl of the watercress soup,
followed by the asparagus and the *mousseline*. Both the
crème de cresson and the *mousseline* have been highly rec-
ommended by reliable sources. As a second course, we
intend to move on to the *boudin de homard* and the *langoustines,* and conclude with the *daurade* and the *homard
aux châtaignes.* You can never put away too much lobster.

Thus prepared, I merely glance up. The captain steps
forward from his position, near the serving station,
where he can observe all nine of his tables. He holds a
small pad at the ready.

"Would it be possible . . . ," I begin in French.

"Yes," the captain breaks in politely. "Whatever it
may be, it is possible."

He assures us that the soup, and any other course,

may be divided in two. Because the *mousseline* has asparagus, however, he suggests that we omit the *asperges au jus de truffes.* I propose the escargots in its stead. The captain nods: first the soup, "as an *amuse-bouche,*" he adds, an indication that the soup will be on the house, followed by the escargots, followed by the *mousseline,* all divided in two. And if we would like the *daurade* and the *homard aux châtaignes,* the captain suggests forgoing, for reasons of volume, the *boudin* and the *langoustines.* What we have overlooked in our gluttony is that any plate divided in two in the kitchen is not truly one half of one serving. In fact, primarily for reasons of aesthetics, a *demi,* or "half," is much closer to a full serving. Each *demi* is prepared separately as a slightly smaller (or in some cases, like that of the *boudin,* no smaller) variation on a full plate. Thus, we will each be served three appetizers and a main course, to say nothing of the gougères, or of the cheese and the desserts to follow. An additional dish apiece, the captain knows, divided or no, would prove uncomfortable, if not physiologically improbable, to consume. No need to overdo it, he might say, but doesn't.

Indeed one must, objects the ghost of A. J. Liebling. In his 1959 classic *Between Meals,* Liebling recounts his apprenticeship in Paris in the 1920s. Lunch for the younger, lighter Liebling, a cub reporter, boxing aficionado, and "eater in training," might consist of *truite au bleu, daube provençale,* and young roasted guinea hens with asparagus, followed by cheese and dessert. With barefaced adulation, he presents numerous accounts of those prize heavyweights of the table, capable of consuming, for example, two cassoulets, a steak with beef marrow, and a dozen or more oysters at a sitting. He reports that the celebrated Yves Mirande, a playwright and gourmand to whom the book is dedicated, once lunched on "raw Bayonne ham and fresh figs, a hot sausage in crust, spindles of filleted pike in a rich rose *sauce Nantua,* a leg of lamb larded with anchovies, artichokes on a pedestal of *fois gras,* and four or five kinds of cheese, with a good bottle of Bordeaux and one of Champagne." Mirande, a small man then in his eighties, was only ramping up. For dinner a few hours hence, he dispatched "larks and ortolans (buntings) . . . with a few *langoustes* (crayfish) and a turbot—and of course, a fine *civet* (or stew) made from the *marcassin,* or young wild boar."

We accept the captain's counsel, and close the door, with regret, on the *boudin* and the *langoustines.* He returns to the serving station and gives a carbon copy of the order to a *commis,* or assistant, who will take it to the kitchen and place it directly into the hands of the chef. I lean back into the banquette with a sensation of relief. It is done. Out of our sight, a machine of near-legendary precision has been set in motion.

In my childhood home, an elegant but sagging white Victorian overlooking the Hudson River in Rockland County, New York, the dining-room table was the heart of things. Which is odd, because when I was a child I never thought much about food. Like sex, money, and the movies, food was something my family didn't dis-

cuss. You could talk freely about religion, history, politics, theater, but food was off the table. We weren't
wealthy, but until I came along, the youngest of four by
a good deal, ours was an academic and well-traveled
family that took its dinner conversation seriously. In
bits and pieces, I learned more at that table than in one
public and three private schools put together. My
parents might have been emotionally repressed intellec-
tuals, but they weren't snobs. Neither had been raised
with money to speak of, and they didn't care a whit
about impressing their guests. My father was often
just as happy to offend them, for he rarely censored his
opinions. He had little interest in avoiding religion and
politics at social gatherings—quite the reverse. Not
to cause discomfort, I believe (having watched this
process many times), nor to sour the event, but in the
bullheaded and unspoken belief that ideas matter, and
we're all grownups, so let's stop mincing around. Not
everyone agreed, and more than once people stormed
up and out of dining rooms after explosive interchanges
with my father over something as seemingly innocuous
as Freud (against) or Kipling (for). My father never
held a grudge that I noted, or took personal offense
when attacked, and somehow he never seemed to learn
that others—including his wife and children—could
or would. My parents talked for the plain love of art and
history and literature above all, and if it is possible to
talk about these subjects at length and in detail without
pretense, they did so. My father bullied and my mother
sulked, but after nearly sixty years of marriage their

conversation hasn't flagged. When we visit them in Washington, we'll come home after a movie and find the two of them by the fire, playing dominoes across the marble coffee table, its underside still covered with the polychrome graffiti of my early childhood, gabbing away about Shaw as if they'd just met that afternoon. After years of recrimination and withdrawal, they have also started flirting again, to the befuddlement and shy delight of their children. They will hold hands, and my father will observe now and again that he married his heart's desire. My sister, who lives near them and visits more frequently, often finds them snuggling—her word—on the couch. It was talk that got them there, that shored up their marriage when all else seemed to have fallen away. If I could wish one thing for any marriage—mine, for instance—it would be this undying love of conversation and ideas. More than true, long-term sexual compatibility, more even than shared opinions on the raising of children. The thing most to be feared in a marriage is the silence, the grey waste of nothing more to say.

In any case, food was considered unintellectual by my family, and thus dull. Worse, it was of the body. We might as well have talked about our bodily waste. Food, it seemed, was either safe, drab, and forgettable (frozen peas and mashed potatoes with a pork chop) or complex, exotic, threatening. What I would now call real food reeked of the passions, of excess, of all the things the careful, well-considered life might fall prey to. Such an association is as old as civilization west of the

Euphrates. The apple was our undoing, not the snake. In the Sayings of the Desert Fathers, Saint Macarius meets the Devil on the road in Egypt, and hails "Whither away, Malignant?" The Tempter is going down to the monastery to harass the brethren, he explains to the future saint, and he does not carry political pamphlets or sheet music under his arm. Hanging from holes in his coat are jars of relish with which to tempt their appetites. "If one does not serve," he tells Macarius, "I try another."

My father was less aloof from dietary matters than my mother, who found cooking and eating an inconvenience if not an affront to womankind, and once said she would happily take all her nourishment in a capsule. So he and I would sneak out together from time to time and eat properly. When I was little, we would go to a hushed, dark little diner called the Wooden Indian on Route 59 in Nyack, New York. There was a big wooden cigar-shop Indian when you came in, standing there like a bouncer, and for years my image of American Indians was formed by that wooden Indian, and by the image of the aging warrior in that era's well-known television commercial against littering. In the spot, as I remember it, the Indian sits on horseback at the edge of the trees above a highway, surrounded by litter, and stonily watches six or eight lanes of cars streaming along in their own haze, a tear on his cheek.

My father and I would sit at the counter of the Wooden Indian and eat cheeseburgers with root beer, followed by vanilla milkshakes made with real ice cream. It was a classic little diner, if a bit solemn. Later, our town's first McDonald's opened just up the street, in walking distance of the Wooden Indian. This was before McDonald's, deservedly perhaps, became a dirty word in parts of America. We were still fighting the Vietnam War, and no one knew what McDonald's would ultimately do to the small American town. It just seemed like a good, clean, cheerful place to get a hamburger. I vividly remember the debut of the Big Mac, and I'm sorry to say that at my insistence we abandoned the Wooden Indian in its favor. The twin patties of the Big Mac may have been scanty, but for an eight-year-old suburban American palate, McDonald's Special Sauce was better than Escoffier's béarnaise. The Wooden Indian was largely occupied by dour middle-aged men, smoking cigarettes behind their newspapers, and though the Indian himself was impressive, he was intimidating, and I never got a mug to take home. McDonald's, we discovered, was always jammed with other kids, and with all the toys and gleeful birthday-party imagery (they even had their own *clown*), why would a little kid want to eat anywhere else? Thanks to us and others like us, the Wooden Indian has long since gone the way of the buffalo, but that same McDonald's remains. I haven't eaten a hamburger in years, but when I drive dazedly through my old hometown, reeling in grief and nostalgia, every street and corner laden with memories, layered one upon another, so thick I can scarcely recall the present day—am I six, am I nine, am I fourteen?—I sometimes stop at McDonald's for old times' sake and eat a fish sandwich and a pocket of fries in a corner booth. I try to remember why it was so exciting to come there with my father long ago, just the two of us. It's invariably noisy and depressing, and I leave feeling cheapened, nagged by fast-food guilt and hot with revived shame for abandoning the Wooden Indian, for letting that good little diner go down.

I suppose it was from my father that I learned to appreciate the well-made American sandwich. Though the best panini in Italy are unforgettable, there is nothing quite like a really good sandwich made in an American home or delicatessen. It may not have originated on these shores, but the sandwich is an American creature: handy, eclectic, generous. The easy portability of the sandwich made it the meal of choice in childhood. We often rode our bikes along the Hudson River, riding all day, and en route we would stop at a local deli near my elementary school, the same deli, still open though in different hands, where I bought my very first stick of Bazooka Bubble Gum for one cent while walking home from kindergarten in 1971. We would order huge Italian subs loaded with salami, pepperoni, and provolone, with shredded iceberg lettuce and onions and oil and vinegar, wrapped up tight and halved through the paper and wrapped again, with a cold bottle of orange soda and a bag of chips. We would wrap the tops of our brown bags around our handlebars, secured beneath our closed fists, and as we pedaled along the bags would swing to and fro, occasionally bouncing against an upraised knee. Somewhere along the trail up north of

Hook Mountain we would find a concrete ruin, or a stone hikers' cabin, and, leaving our bikes by the trail, we would explore the structure and eat our sandwiches, the oil and vinegar running out of them. The woman who owned the deli had a free hand. I loved opening the wrapped sandwich, cracking it like a book, and inspecting its layered and perfectly bisected faces, neat as if cut with a straight razor.

Somewhere about that time, I decided that I did not like deli sandwiches made by men. If there was an unpleasant incident I don't recall it, but I determined that if females were inherently clean, and so I believed them to be, males were inherently unclean. I had the very definite sense that there was nothing that might appear on the hands of a woman, especially a young woman, that could soil her. In turn, I believed that even the most vigorous hand-washing could never quite remove the essential uncleanliness of the young man. I failed to remember, in this equation, or did not fully know, that one of the many things that might cross the hands of a young woman was a young man. There were erotic overtones, to be sure, in this fixation on the female sandwich, but the issue was primarily emotional. To eat a sandwich made by a girl was somehow like being caressed. If I stopped at an unknown deli and there was a young man behind the counter, I would with disappointment satisfy myself with a candy bar or a bag of chips. This continues to a lesser degree to this day: I still take distinct pleasure in the female sandwich, and only with great force of will am I able to overcome my distaste for the male sandwich. If the young man is wearing those absurd rubber gloves it helps, but if the young woman is wearing them I feel robbed, as if I am being deprived of an essential and mysterious ingredient. Oddly enough, I do not feel this way at all with professional cooks. While working in a kitchen, where I know the cooks, I have no problem eating food prepared by men. It is strictly a stranger-in-a-deli kind of thing, but it remains. One summer, in the deepest throes of this particular mania, I developed a debilitating crush on a girl of fifteen who worked at the small deli in Menemsha, Massachusetts. Though I never did manage to ask her out, a blunder I have never forgiven, you can be assured I ate a good many of her sandwiches. I would ask her for recommendations, or to make me her own favorites, and I would stand at the counter and watch her prepare them, ingredient by ingredient, and when she would unconsciously lick her fingers after treating them with dressing or mayonnaise, I would go weak in the legs. My favorite sandwich at that deli was a big hot sandwich on light rye called the Ivan. Roast beef, melted Swiss cheese, onion, and Russian dressing. Her name was Katie.

For his part, my father does not share my distaste for the male sandwich, which is a good thing, for I like making them. It is particularly satisfying to make sandwiches for my father, because he eats them with such gusto. He can eat a sandwich on a moment's notice, at any time. He bends over the plate and demolishes the sandwich in great bites, sitting back up to chew, and all the while making appreciative noises. My mother, for her part, favors quartered watercress or cucumber sandwiches on white bread with a little glaze of mayonnaise and trimmed crusts. They can be tasty, too, but they are not sandwiches as I understand them. They are hors d'oeuvres, at which my mother is an expert. Although my mother does not care much for family cooking, she loves to entertain.

My relationship with my mother and food came to a memorable head one summer afternoon in suburbia. I was eleven or twelve, and she had called me in to lunch in the midst of an important game—an adaptation of *Rollerball,* a violent science-fiction film of the time, played on bikes and skateboards with a lacrosse ball and what amounted, when all the abrasions and bruises were tallied, to full contact on asphalt. The very last thing I wanted to do at such a time was come inside and eat one of my mother's lunches. So I protested. I sat in front of the dry peanut-butter-and-jelly sandwich and the tall glasses of milk and tomato juice and determined not to eat a bite. My father wasn't home, or he would have made short work of me. My mother, to her credit, stood fast on this particular occasion and would not be cowed. No lunch, no Roller Ball. More than an hour passed. The rattling crash of bicycles, the rasp of skateboard wheels skudding across blacktop, and the groans of the wounded wafted mercilessly across the lawn. Finally, my mother proposed an alternative. Would it be easier, she asked, if she threw it all in a blender? Then I could simply drink it down and be done with it.

I nodded. Away went the lunch, and back came a blender and a glass. I poured out the first, full serving, closed my eyes, and took a sip. The acid in the tomato juice, the curdling milk, the chunks of crust, and the oily globs of peanut butter gave this mélange all the tang and texture of real vomit. In color, taste, and consistency it was absolutely impossible to distinguish from the genuine article. The second tall glass was harder than the first, but I got it down.

I should point out that I hold myself equally responsible for this incident, and others like it. And though my mother stood at odds with family cooking, she often did her best. I remember with particular pleasure our Sunday-morning ritual, when all of us would gather for breakfast on my parents' king-sized bed. My mother would come up with a tray laden with croissants, scrambled eggs, juice, and grapefruit. While the morning sun came across the Hudson River and through the leaded windows, we would lounge and eat and read in our pajamas, sprawled out across the bed like a pride of lions. In such moments, one might have thought us an ideal family, and indeed, in such moments, we were.

Parenting now is largely the process of selection. Of carefully unbraiding the mixed experience of our childhoods, finding again all the wonderful things our parents did for us, large and small, and preserving them, passing them on. I am teaching our daughter to read in precisely the same way that my father taught me. We curl up in bed in the mornings and go through the same McGuffey Reader, lesson by lesson. I study the black-

and-white images I have not seen for thirty years, and I can feel my father's warmth beside me, always on my left in the big bed, as surely as I feel the warmth of my daughter, curled up beside me on my right.

In Taillevent, I drain the last of Erin's cocktail and set the glass with unconscious finality on the cloth in front of me. The empty Kir glass has already vanished, borne away by a server with the deftness of a pickpocket while we considered our menus. Now, at precisely the right moment, the glass goblet is whisked from the table. An instant too soon, and it would suggest that the server had been watching, and is hurrying us. An instant too late, and I might become aware that the glass, now empty, should be cleared away—that we are not being *quite* as well taken care of as we might be. Of these, the second is certainly the lesser evil. Even the vaguest sense of hurry—observed in the waiting staff, or imposed, with greater or lesser subtlety, upon the dinner guests—is death to a fine meal. It is far better for a waiter to be somewhat too phlegmatic—in taking orders, pouring wine, clearing plates—than too quick. At table, as in life, hurry is the great destroyer of happiness and sound work, and more insidious even than laziness or lack of care. It splinters the mind and breeds impatience, and in its later stages panic, and unravels all.

The empty goblet rests on the table for three or four beats—long enough for me to retract my hand, sever my mind from its ownership, and direct my attention elsewhere, but not so long that the glass regains my attention, on the next pass of the eye, as an empty glass, as clutter. Precisely then, swift but unhurried, it is lifted by a man in a white jacket, *en passant*, and floats away.

Le Vin

At 9:00, the *chef sommelier* pauses at the serving station, scans our order with a fingertip, and moves to our table. He is tall and pale, with lively, intelligent eyes in a drawn face. He cannot be much over thirty, and with his pallid skin against his dark hair and black jacket, and the arrestingly elegant, flat black apron that reaches nearly to his shoes, he cuts a romantic and somehow tragic figure—a matador, perhaps, or a consumptive Russian painter. He could be Raskolnikov.

Since my first, threadbare trip to France at nineteen, I have harbored a nostalgic fondness for the bottles of contestably undrinkable Côtes du Rhône sold at Arab markets throughout Paris. If I am not a foodie, I am even less an expert on wine, and though I enjoy a good wine as much as the next man, I could not distinguish an Haut Médoc from a Pomerol under torture. Accordingly, I ask the sommelier for advice.

"These days, many people are ordering red wine with fish," he says. "You could do that. There are a number of reds that would go very well." He pauses, then adds, *"C'est très à la mode."* From his tone, perfectly polite but neutral, it is hard to tell if he is daring us to order a red, or shaming us against it. In comportment, like the fleet of *maîtres d'hôtel*, the sommelier manages to appear both perfectly relaxed and flawlessly mannered. He exudes an air of absolute competence without hauteur.

"What would you order?" I dodge.

He muses. "A white Burgundy, perhaps." The wine list offers some four hundred French wines from twelve regions, including Bordeaux, Champagne, Burgundy, Côtes du Rhône, Alsace, and the Loire. There is not a single foreign bottle on the list. No Chilean Médocs, no Californian Chardonnays, no Australian Wullabuggas. The sommelier indicates two white Burgundies in the neighborhood of three or four hundred francs, out of a list that ranges in cost from less than thirty dollars a bottle, to a 1989 Le Montrachet for twenty-two hundred francs, or some $370. The most expensive wine of any kind is a 1937 Pomerol from Château Nenin for fifty-eight hundred francs, or nearly a thousand dollars a bottle.

"Could I give you a general price range?" I ask with some embarrassment. "We'd like to have a really good wine, and might prefer a half-bottle of something better, if you follow me."

"Absolutely," says the sommelier, furrowing his brow in a nod of comprehension. "I understand perfectly. It's quite natural."

"Something, I don't know, in the neighborhood of six hundred francs?" About a hundred dollars. I can feel the heat in my face, from the two apéritifs, from my vinicultural illiteracy, and from the suspicion that I have just committed the evening's first unspeakable act: discussing money. Although I have often felt each emotion singly, for the first time in memory I feel simultaneously cheap and ostentatious.

He nods, ponders the list for a moment as I study him. I try to determine if he's lying, if my inquiry was not natural at all. He is poised and inscrutable. "I believe this would be suitable," he says, and indicates a 1993 Chevalier-Montrachet, Domaine Leflaive, priced at a thousand francs for a full bottle. A half would be less than a hundred dollars.

"I don't have the '93 in a half," the sommelier continues, "but I have the '92. It is a very, very good wine."

Wedged between the villages of Puligny-Montrachet and Chassagne-Montrachet, three kilometers southwest of Meursault, the vineyards of Chevalier-Montrachet and those of Bâtard-Montrachet border those of Le Montrachet proper. All three are *grands crus* (literally "great growth"), which is to say wines of the highest rank. The wine produced by Le Montrachet, marginally superior to that of its two neighbors, is regarded by many to be the finest and most complex white wine in the world. The vines of Chevalier-Montrachet grow in stonier soil than those of Le Montrachet, and thus produce a wine that is more delicate. Bâtard-Montrachet lies in turn on richer ground, and its wines are generally said to lack some of Montrachet's finesse.

When the sommelier has taken his leave, the second *maître d'hôtel* appears and asks us if we would prefer flat or carbonated water. Though fervent admirers of the bubbly, intensely mineral Badoit, neither of us is in the mood for anything that forward here. Flat, we reply, and before we can specify a brand, Volvic is poured immediately from a glass bottle.

This seemingly inconsequential detail has considerable impact, a final augur that we are in capable hands. The fact that we were given no choice is not lost on us, a sure indication that Monsieur Vrinat and his staff believe with some certainty, as we do, that Volvic is the best bottled flat water available. Other candidates all taste a little off by comparison, and the soapy Évian is the worst of the breed. They do have Évian on hand, for demanding masochists, and Badoit, and Vittel, and a number of others, for they are prepared to please all tastes. But Volvic is the water they serve.

Hippocrates specified that the best drinking water is "clear, light, inodorous, without any flavor, and drawn from springs exposed to the east." Nearer to Volvic, that is, than to Évian. Pliny wrote that "fleece spread about [a] ship, after having received the exhalations from the sea, becomes damp, and fresh water may be extracted from it." For a period of history on Iron Island (Ferro, of the Canaries), the sole source of fresh water was sea vapor collected from the leaves of a forty-foot tree called the garoë. So consistent was the flow of vapor in that part of the island that water ran like rain from the tree's boughs and broad leaves. Collected in two stone cisterns, tended and distributed by a guard, the water so gathered provided sufficiently, we are told, for the island's eight thousand human and hundred thousand bovine inhabitants. This precipitating tree was destroyed by a whirlwind in 1625; where the

islanders and their cattle turned for water after this sin-
gular calamity is unknown. If they had raised sheep
instead of cows—an unforeseeable error—they could
have taken a cue from Pliny's seafarers. Each shepherd
could have been allotted a set time of each day to trot
his herd of black-legged sponges across that humid
acre. Sloshing home, the woolen beasts could have been
herded sequentially through a large, rotating press built
of garoë wood, and wrung out harmlessly, one after
another, over a barrel. But the Iron Islanders were stuck
with short-haired cattle, of little more use than pigs for
harvesting water. They probably dug a well.

In the cellar, a crackling voice erupts from a loud-
speaker. "Chevalier-Montrachet, '92, *demi*." In a small,
brightly lit room at the foot of the stairs, another *maître
d'hôtel* is preparing cheeses. His post is here, in this
room, throughout the service. Along one wall, glass-
doored coolers and refrigerators are stocked with butter, cheese, bottled water. Silver ice buckets are stacked
under a counter, beside the thrumming ice machine.
Another man—the *caviste,* who hunts down the wines—
confirms reception of the order through the intercom
and moves down the narrow corridor at a trot. He con-
sults a hanging chart. There are hundreds of thousands
of bottles laid down in the cellars of Taillevent, and he
could not possibly recall the locations of every château,
every vintage. He scans the list, finds it, then runs back
down the corridor. He pushes through a steel doorway
into a large cell. The air in the cell is cooler than in the
corridor, at sixteen degrees Celsius, and faintly damp. It

is floored with gravel. Periodically, the floor is sprayed with water. The gravel allows the moisture to evaporate gradually and humidify the air, which helps preserve the corks. The wine is laid on tightly spaced wooden shelves, floor to ceiling. Thanks to the sustained efforts, over decades, of Vrinat and his sommeliers, this is beyond reasonable doubt the finest wine cellar in the world. Notorious for perfectionism and micromanagement of every facet of his enterprise, Vrinat has long given special attention to his *cave*. Throughout his career, he has bought more than two million bottles of wine. The *caviste* dodges left, then right, his shoes crunching on the stones. The Chevalier-Montrachet is in the corner, near the floor, in section 622 *bis*, a row of bottles glazed in dust. He seizes a half-bottle, marks the day's date and the number of bottles remaining on a card that stays with the stock, and dashes back to the small room. He dusts the bottle thoroughly with a clean rag and sets it in a bucket of ice and water. An assistant server in a white jacket appears and runs it upstairs.

At 9:12, the captain sets two bowls of *crème de cresson* before us. As an *amuse-bouche* that will not appear on the bill, the soup is a flourish, he explains, *quelque chose de plus*. The *crème de cresson* feels like a stroke of unexpected fortune, like finding a five-hundred-franc note in the fine gravel of the Place Dauphine. Late at night, I sometimes stand in the center of this square, hands in coat pockets, as if age and light and geometry alone might provide, if one is sufficiently patient, some consolation deeper than might be found in living company.

Le Vin

If the great *jardins* are the open-air cathedrals of secular Paris, her small squares, especially when abandoned, are her chapels, and many a foreigner has betrothed himself to that city, not at the summit of the Tour Eiffel, or at a sidewalk table at the Café de Flore, but while sitting alone on a cold bench in a damp empty square late at night. In any case, there, beside the bench, one might conceivably find a folded, faintly rumpled banknote—five hundred francs. The nearest equivalent, in French currency, to the hundred-dollar bill. You would scan the square, half expecting to find a greying gentleman of commerce hurrying back from his Citroën in your direction. There is no possible claimant in view; it is yours. It must have escaped inaudibly as its owner, seated on the end of the bench, withdrew keys or handkerchief or cigarette lighter from his trouser pocket. There is the sense that some minor deity of mischief engineered the loss, specifically for your discovery, knowing that you would spend it rashly, regardless of your financial circumstances, on something extravagant and passing, like good wine.

The *crème de cresson* is a crisp, pale green. I lower my spoon slowly into the liquid, allowing the soup to run in a single trickle over the spoon's silver edge. I know that there is something black and shiny in the bowl's depths, but I leave it be. The cream is cool, fresh as cut grass. Sinking from sight, the spoon now penetrates something gelatinous, and resurfaces with a crescent of grey lobster gelatin and caviar. The caviar eggs, the diameter of pinheads, crunch between the teeth. The caviar and lobster gelatin taste like smoke and sea wind. Beside me, my wife makes a sound of appreciation.

"This is delicious," she says. She looks past me. "Do you see that man at the table to your left?" she says, lowering her voice and returning her gaze to her soup. "He has been getting happier and happier." A Frenchman in his sixties, and a woman who appears to be his wife, are in a booth with a younger couple—the couple's daughter and her husband, I suspect. I study the older man; he is leaning into the table, flushed and animated, telling a story. They are well into their main course; a bottle of Bordeaux stands nearly empty on the table. I feel a sudden, filial fondness for this older gentleman, this red-faced, white-haired stranger. I can feel the same contentment awakening and moving through my veins, expanding from my torso, into my face and limbs. Alive, I think. Good God, I know how he feels.

A *maître d'hôtel* approaches the table and asks if we would like to start the wine. We decline, intending to wait for the *entrées*. Three minutes later, when we have nearly finished our soup, the *maître d'* who greeted us at the door appears, smiles broadly, and opens the wine without further inquiry. I cannot tell if this is an error of miscommunication on the part of the floor staff, or if we are being subtly encouraged to follow an established pace.

The first *maître d'* returns, lifts the open bottle from the bucket, glances at the label, and grins. *"J'ai de la chance,"* he says cheerily, "Aren't I lucky," and pours a generous splash into a wineglass. He drains the glass, raises his eyebrows, grins again. *"J'ai beaucoup de chance,"* he says, and pours our wine. Some taste, I think, suppressing my alarm. The guy just tossed back fifty francs. Considered an expression of superior service, protecting as it does the patron's palate from the possible affront of a bad wine, such a policy is commonplace in restaurants of high caliber. Nonetheless, I prefer to taste my own wine, and would rather get a mouthful of vinegar than have someone else decide in my stead. Part of this is knee-jerk, territorial selfishness, and part of it is ingrained self-reliance. Park my own car; fix my own sink; taste my own wine. A neurosis shored up by a virtue.

I thank the *maître d'*, whose enthusiasm for the wine is nevertheless infectious, and raise a toast to my wife. We touch glasses and drink. The wine is full-flavored and complex—tasty, certainly, but not stunning. It has a vague tartness, a faintly excessive edge, like a banjo with one string slightly out of tune, and in my ignorance I wonder if it's simply a little young. Erin is neutral. "It's not bad," she says under her breath, between sips. She is invariably more difficult to please than I am, and can unfailingly distinguish a truly remarkable Camembert, to name one example, from a merely excellent cousin. Not that she is impossible to satisfy; in the privacy of our apartment, she often takes an alarmingly vocal pleasure in foods—strong French cheeses in particular—that pass muster.

In Paris in 1990, at a restaurant in the Seventeenth, a

friend and I shared a half-bottle of 1978 Saint-Émilion La Fleur, and I knew immediately that it was the best wine I had ever tasted. This may say more about the limits of my experience with wines of quality than about the strengths of a wine that does not merit, on the books, a classification of *grand cru classé*. I knew nothing about its official standing; I knew only that it was astonishingly dry and dusty against my tongue and against the insides of my cheeks, and that the sip just floated there in my mouth as if it were a weightless sphere, its fumes rising up and into my nasal passages, so that, when I breathed slowly through my nose, the wine resting in my mouth, my breath was nothing but a sublime vapor. That particular split of Saint-Émilion made it clear to me what wine was capable of—even in a half-bottle—and it changed my palate permanently.

Minutes later, a *maître d'hôtel* lifts the bottle of Chevalier-Montrachet from the ice, dries it, sets it on the table, and removes the stand. As the sommelier later reminds me, wine should never be overchilled. "A great wine must not frost the glass," he says. "The wine must remain clear, limpid. If the outside of the glass beads with moisture, the wine is too cold." Excessive cold flattens the flavor of a wine, as it does with cheese or desserts—even ice cream loses flavor if too cold. An overly chilled wine will revive as its temperature climbs back into its preferred range. Bad wine, like bad beer, can be made less flavorful, and thus more palatable, by overchilling. Beyond laziness and misinformation, this is one reason so many restaurants simply leave your white wine in its bucket until the bottle is empty.

Ten days after our meal, I meet with Taillevent's sommelier, Nicolas Bonnot, in the cheerless grey refectory, or staff dining room, before a dinner shift. Born in 1968 in Aubervilliers, outside Paris, Bonnot came into a family of cooks and restaurateurs. His grandparents owned a restaurant in Orléans, his father is a chef, and his mother works at a Parisian hotel. In lieu of university, he spent two years in trade school. Though he originally planned to become a *chef de cuisine,* he found the kitchen too hot, and he missed the contact with clients. So he decided to work in the dining room. On finishing trade school, he spent two years in Germany, first in a small family hotel near Frankfurt, and later in a French restaurant. It was there that he began to appreciate wine. "I began to work at it," he says. "I had no formal training, but I read, I studied, little by little, and wine became a passion." Two years in England followed, moving from waiter to *maître d'hôtel* to assistant manager. He soon returned to France for a year of obligatory military service, and found employment as a *commis* sommelier at Le Vivarois, a two-star restaurant in the Sixteenth. He then moved to Lucas Carton, on the Place de la Madeleine. Over six years, an astonishing pace, he climbed the ranks through *demi-sommelier* and sommelier to become *chef sommelier* at the three-star restaurant. His knowledge of English and German, he says, helped a great deal. Three years ago, he moved to Taillevent as chef-sommelier. In his current position, he often travels with Vrinat and helps select wines for the *cave*.

"To succeed at this profession," he says, "you must be able to read a client in seconds. When you arrive at a table to take an order, you must immediately determine what he wants and how much he wishes to spend. You must understand why the client is here. If he is here with his wife, or with his mistress, he will have a very different manner. The sommelier must be patient, available, attentive. It requires psychology, and a great deal of technique. He must be a professional who knows his trade. And he must not want to give lessons. That's the most important thing—he must know how to listen to the client."

Bonnot claims that his exchange with clients is the most rewarding aspect of his work. "Clients will often ask if I know such-and-such a wine, and often I say no. I learn more from my clients each day."

I ask if it is indeed acceptable to give a price range to the sommelier.

"Absolutely," he says. "It's difficult when one is less familiar with the country, or with the restaurant. I find it perfectly natural to say, 'This is what I can spend; what do you recommend in that range?'" I watch him again for signs of diplomatic deceit, but can still see nothing beyond his amicable, balanced gaze. Bonnot is not one I would care to face across a card table.

Smaller bottles, he explains, can adversely affect a wine as it ages. Half-bottles will mature more rapidly, a condition that is generally more problematic with reds than whites. To counter this, Taillevent tries to serve half-bottles of younger wines, where there is little or no difference in quality. This is made easier by the fact that viniculture has trended toward younger wines in recent years. "In the forties, fifties, and sixties," says Bonnot, "it was impossible to imagine drinking a Bordeaux younger than twenty or twenty-five years. Now the technique has so progressed that we can produce early-maturing wines to be drunk in three, four, five years. We're drinking lighter and lighter wines, with fruitier flavors. We're drinking more champagne, more apéritifs. On the other hand, we're drinking far fewer *digestifs*. The *digestif* has all but disappeared."

In recent years, Bonnot has seen a marked advance in the wines of certain regions, including those of Burgundy, Provence, Languedoc, and Côtes du Rhône. Historically, Côtes du Rhônes have been very potent. Now, he says, they are becoming more aromatic, more delicate, more balanced. "On the other hand," he says, "the wines of Bordeaux have become more and more standardized. Now, in Bordeaux, it's difficult to have any feeling for the wines."

"The climate, the land in which it is grown, the angle of the land to the sun, the quality of the soil, the age of the vines—all these factors are important in the creation of a great wine," he says later. "Equally important is the influence of human will. To produce a great wine, one must ally nature to man. Man must interpret nature. You need a great piece of land, with old vines, but the vintner must understand his vines. If he does not, even if the environment is perfect, the wine will be worthless."

L'Entrée

Behind the service station, down a dim, carpeted corridor, stand two pairs of automatic doors. They divide the dining room from the kitchen like an air lock. Beyond the doors, the corridor, now bright and tiled in grey, continues past a lone dishwasher in a pale-blue shirt and navy apron, loading plates and glasses into racks for his machines. This dishwasher (two others scrub pots in a washroom beyond the stoves) is short, middle-aged, and wears the permanent scowl of the downtrodden. He seldom raises his eyes, even when addressed. The corridor opens into the kitchen's service area, equipped with an espresso machine and an automated dumbwaiter. Slips of paper go up on the dumbwaiter, and desserts come down. The service area is divided from the stoves and the *brigade* that works them by a steel counter, covered by a soft, fitted white cloth. Above the counter is a row of heat lamps. Under the lamps, steel plate-covers lean in stacks beside a tray of gougères. Chef Philippe Legendre stands at the end of the counter. When the assistant server hands him our order, Legendre glances down at the slip and calls out in a flat, booming voice that carries clearly over the clattering assembly: *"Deux couverts; deux demi cresson; deux demi escargots; deux demi mousselines; homard; daurade!"*

Without looking up from his present task—the injection of sauce into a trio of *cannellonis de tourteau* with a culinary hypodermic that could only look at home in the laboratory of Young Frankenstein—a young *commis,* or assistant cook, replies, *"Oui, chef,"* in a small voice. He is bent over a counter in the *garde-manger,* the cold-food preparation area behind Legendre. Many of the older, more confident members of the *brigade* sing out simply "Chef!" by way of confirming an order. This *commis,* Stephane DuMans, has only been at Taillevent for two months, and he is not about to shout abbreviations at Legendre, a major figure in the culinary pantheon of France. The *commis* is the first paid position in the kitchen, senior only to the apprentice. From that level, a young cook will mount to *demi-chef de partie, chef de partie, premier* or *second sous-chef,* and finally, for the rare few, *chef de cuisine.* The nearest English equivalent to *chef de partie* is "line cook."

The kitchen is divided into five stations, or departments, each with its own cooks and assistants. *Garde-manger* is the first station, followed by *entremets* (vegetables and soups), *rotisseur* (poultry and beef), *poisson* (fish), and the fifth and most critical station, *sauces.* Commonly, cooks move gradually up from the first station, gaining experience in all departments as their seniority accrues. The current saucier is Legendre's *second sous-chef,* Christophe Guibert. A cook of indubitable skill, Guibert would also make a good café waiter of the kind feared by Americans, for his default expression hovers in that disconcerting and uniquely Gallic province between the smirk and the sneer.

Legendre turns to the end of the *garde-manger* counter behind him and presses the slip onto a corkboard. Barred with ragged strips of two-sided adhesive tape, the board is quilted with *commandes,* or orders. Many of the items on the slips have been marked with pink checks by the station chefs of the *garde-manger,* indicating that they have prepared a portion of meat or fish and passed it to the chefs at the stoves.

Head down, his chin against the knot of his white kerchief, Legendre studies the board, calls out a reminder, moves slips into new positions. The corkboard is a shifting puzzle, Legendre's means of assuring that each *entrée* and *plat* is served exactly when it must be served. The ideal time, he tells me, between the placement of the order and the delivery of the appetizer is ten minutes. Knowing something of Vrinat, I suspect this is timed to the second.

Legendre turns back to face the covered counter. A *commis* from the *entremets* places two plates of asparagus on a wooden tray before him. The asparagus are firm, brilliant green, bathed in a coppery broth, and sprinkled with minute dice of black truffle. A white cloth hangs from the waist of Legendre's apron; he takes it up with his right hand, wraps a corner of it around his forefinger, and dips it into a small metal bowl of diluted brown vinegar that rests on the counter's edge. Spinning the plates in place with his left hand, he polishes the white rim of each plate to a high shine with the dampened cloth. The diluted vinegar adds brilliance. Then he caps the plates with steel covers, recently warmed on the stove by Legendre himself, and calls to an approaching server, *"Table treize!"*

During a service, Legendre does not cook, any more than an eighteenth-century admiral would have loaded carronades under fire. Legendre is the mind and voice of the kitchen; its hands are the members of his meticulously trained *brigade*. After creating or adapting a dish, usually with the help of his second, Alain Davy, he instructs his staff in its production. Operating at their respective stations, his *chefs de partie,* and to a lesser extent their *commis,* must know precisely how each dish must look and taste. This requires not only impeccable technique and close attention but a well-trained palate. Though his cooks cannot be expected to have palates quite the match of his own, they must be able to reproduce unfailingly—day after day, service after service, at speed and under intense pressure—exactly what he calls for. Rarely, Legendre will taste a sauce, dipping a spoon into its copper pot. Guibert seldom errs. In my time there, weeks scattered across a three-month period, Legendre has found fault with a sauce only once, and then mildly; other cooks are less fortunate— *"Non! Non! Non! Merde! Ça me fait chier!"* ("No! No! No! Shit! That pisses me off!")—but even this is rare. All in all, it seems a well-trained, disciplined, and contented crew.

In preparation for a lunch or dinner service, in the mornings and afternoons, Legendre will perform some of the kitchen's simplest, apprentice-level tasks, often in the company of Davy. Close friends who have worked together for fourteen years, they stand together at the polished counter of the *garde-manger* and meditatively dice truffles or probe trays of fresh crabmeat with their fingertips for flecks of shell. The two chefs work in silence or chat in barely audible voices, while their underlings carry out what might be called the expert work: preparing the sauces, the soups, the fish and meats. To some degree, I suspect Legendre and Davy do this work because their hands are free, and their *chefs de partie* cannot as easily be spared. For another, although they might not be conscious of it, there may be something restorative in these simple, repetitive acts, a return to the craft's headwaters.

The simplest things, of course, are often the most difficult to master. In many French cooking schools, one of the first lessons is the perfect omelet. This is not something you are guaranteed to learn in a day, or even a week, but you will learn, because you will not run out of eggs. If there is the faintest hint of browning on the omelet, to begin with, it is rejected, and the student starts again. Joël Robuchon believes his finest recipe to be his mashed potatoes. I have not tasted them, but they are rumored to be to ordinary mashed potatoes what Michelangelo's *Pietà* is to a hastily fashioned snowman. The recipe requires very simple steps involving three or four ingredients: potatoes, salt, butter, perhaps a little milk. One evening, I am told, Robuchon's *sous-chef*, a highly skilled chef in his own right, prepared the mashed potatoes, as he had countless times before, and brought a bowl to Robuchon for his approval. The chef tasted the result and pushed it back across the counter with an almost imperceptible grimace. "If you do it right from the beginning," he said simply, "you will never have a problem." He left his confounded protégé to think it over.

In any case, Legendre's involvement with such simple tasks underscores what I imagine to be a subtle but invaluable point—the chef is not above working beside his crew. During the service, Legendre's post is at the corkboard and the service counter. The counter is his transom, the final point of contact and approval. From this surface his creations vanish, borne away on the shoulders of those uneasy allies, the servers, to be delivered into the hands of the unseen.

Dead neutral at first glance, Legendre's expression in the kitchen carries elements of real or affected boredom, in the drooping flatness around the mouth, and of disdain, in the faintly arching brows. Together these give him a somewhat sulky and superior aspect; he looks like someone who feels insufficiently appreciated for his talents, and, relatedly, as if he considers his tenure at Taillevent to be slumming. There is a quality to his expression that one might expect to see in the face of a high-ranking Napoleonic cavalry officer obliged by his English captors to walk.

Legendre was born in May of 1958 in the rural town of Les Essarts, in the department of the Vendée, in western France. His father and grandfather were upholstery designers; his mother was a housewife who later owned a furniture store. Legendre discovered an instinct for cooking as a child, inspired first by a grandmother, later by a great-aunt in the neighboring Loire-Atlantique, who lived in a mill and cooked at a nearby château. By the age of twelve, Legendre often cooked for his parents and three sisters.

He left school and completed his first culinary apprenticeship at seventeen, under the direction of a master chef in nearby Saint-Gilles-Croix-de-Ville. A year later, in 1976, he came to Paris, and worked for a year and a half in the kitchen of the Hotel Sheraton, his first six months as a butcher's boy. It is difficult to envision one so thoroughly in control of his element, so comfortable in his authority, as a tentative neophyte. Imagining Legendre in DuMans's position, submitting his first, flawed efforts to the chef of the Sheraton not quite a quarter-century before, is a bit like conjuring up the young Horatio Nelson on his first ship, when the future rear admiral and tactical genius hardly knew a jib from a jackstay.

Following his tenure at the Sheraton, Legendre spent an obligatory year in the army. On his release, he returned briefly to the Sheraton, did a short tour at Lucas Carton, and spent two years at the Ritz, where he flourished under the direction of Chef Guy Legay. When he arrived at the Ritz at the age of twenty-one, there were fifty-five-year-old *chefs de partie* in the kitchen. At that time in France, Legendre tells me, it was not unusual for cooks to work as long as forty years in the same restaurant. Since the posts of chef and *sous-chef* were rarely vacated, many cooks with promise chose to remain *chefs de partie* for decades, rather than move to another restaurant in search of promotion. The result, of course, was a tight and highly seasoned kitchen. This is no longer the case, says Legendre; the enormous number of restaurants in contemporary France encourages frequent moves and rapid advancement. The mean level of competence in the industry has diminished apace.

At twenty-three, Legendre arrived at Taillevent and assumed the post of *chef de partie* at the *rotisseur*. From there he advanced to *chef de partie au poisson*, and thence to *sous-chef* under then chef Claude Deligne. Legendre was promoted to chef upon Deligne's retirement in 1992. To date, the crowning moment of Legendre's career came in 1996, when he was awarded Meilleur Ouvrier de France. As part of a national competition held every four years, Legendre prepared many dishes over a period of two months and joined some seven hundred French artisans who have been awarded the title in all fields.

Vrinat, Legendre, and Gilles Bajolle decide upon the restaurant's menus, and Legendre may resent Bajolle's unusual degree of influence. In most cases, as part of a chef's larger *équipe*, the pastry chef is considered an underling. A chef may ordinarily refer to "my pastry chef." Whatever Legendre's and Bajolle's respective positions on paper, Bajolle appears to answer directly to Vrinat, making him closer to a peer than a senior member of Legendre's staff. I suspect that Vrinat welcomes and abets Bajolle's prominence, not only for his proven ability, but aiding, as it may, to keep Legendre in check. Unsurprisingly, the rapport between the chefs is not without strain. The two men have known each other since 1976, when Legendre was a *commis*, and they worked together for a year at the Ritz in 1979. Legendre, well aware of Bajolle's talent, brought him over to Taillevent when he was promoted to chef. Such friction aside, their mutual admiration is evident. Legendre, while scarcely able to conceal his loathing of his employer, is clearly happy to have Bajolle upstairs. "It's a good nut," he says of the collection of cooks in the two kitchens. In the peach that is Taillevent, he explains, the nut, or the pit, is the *brigade*. "If the pit rots," he says, "the peach rots."

A few weeks before our dinner at the restaurant, I asked Legendre if he worried about his Michelin ranking. The award or retraction of one or more Michelin stars in the French culinary world is well known to be a major—indeed, pivotal—event for any restaurant. If Taillevent were to be docked a star, the event would be considered a stunning disaster for Vrinat and his staff, and would receive prominent mention in the French press. Legendre was not to be rattled. "Michelin stars," he said, "have never been my objective. My objective is simply to work well." When he arrived at Taillevent, he claimed, he was not even aware of its ranking.

"I cook because it is my profession," he said, "and because I love the work. I like the products, I like a job well done, and I like to give pleasure to the clients. If one doesn't love cooking, one must stop."

He described the difficulty of working in a kitchen where the chef and his staff receive little or no favorable response from their employer, the clients, and the floor staff. The food leaves the kitchen, and stone-faced waiters return.

"There is no relationship," said Legendre. "The food goes out into a vacuum. If the food were bad, I would hear about it. Therefore, I must tell myself that it's fine. It's not easy. It's very hard."

The directness of this admission seemed to pierce his characteristic hauteur. He seemed at a loss, momentarily, like a man who knows that he has a gift, and has tried his best, and can't quite understand why, for as long as he can remember, it has never been good enough. Vrinat suddenly became the driven, brooding father in an immaculate but loveless house, Legendre and Bajolle his two sons, and despite the lavish praise bestowed upon them, justly, by the outside world, I felt a momentary sympathy for this chef at the top of his game. I had heard the same thing, repeatedly and with great frustration, from Bajolle, and could see the effects of Vrinat's enforced silence at a constant simmer in both men.

I asked Legendre if Vrinat's system conspired to draw the best out of his cooks, like that of a football coach who never has a kind word and thus inspires his team to greater excellence.

"The problem is that this is not American football," Legendre replied curtly. "We're feeding people. There is a craft, and a love of craft; there is the talent of all the *garçons.* So it's completely different." He paused. He seemed to be thinking, how to make this American understand that the centuries-old tradition of French cooking can in no way be illuminated through the prism of contact sports. "There is a personal touch in this work," he went on, "an element of love.

"If you don't love others you can't cook," he said. "People who have no love to share eat poorly, and they don't cook. If you love cooking, you *will* cook, at whatever level. People who like to be around a table, who like to share—they'll try to cook, even if it's only an egg. I would much prefer to eat an egg with friends than caviar with strangers. That's important. To be a cook you must love life, you have to like going out into the world. You won't cook well in a cloister. To cook you must be open to others, you must give and receive love."

When DuMans finishes the *cannellonis,* carefully placing the three crab-filled tubes in a fan in a shallow pool of cream-colored sauce and adding a sprig of parsley, he wipes the rim of the plate with a cloth, draws back slightly to inspect the finished dish, and places it on the empty tray before Legendre. Then he hurries worriedly back to his post, and sets two small ceramic bowls on the counter in preparation for the *crème de cresson.* Aged twenty, raised in the Vendôme, DuMans began his career as a sixteen-year-old apprentice while still in *lycée,* the French equivalent of high school. Bespectacled and cheerful, he works swiftly, his head lowered, in a state of nearly tremulous absorption, as if defusing a bomb. Should one of the others creep up behind the young *commis* and shout "DuMans!" for their amusement, he would jump six feet straight up out of his white clogs. Retrieving materials from a refrigerator beneath the counter, he spoons a quarter-inch of black caviar, some fifteen grams, into the bottom of each bowl, followed by enough lobster gelatin to cover the caviar. Then he stirs and ladles in the cream of watercress.

Legendre developed the recipe some six years ago, having pondered the potential of watercress since his days as an apprentice. He tried it with sea urchin, and found that combination wanting. Lobster, known to go well with caviar, had also been matched successfully with watercress—these were established relationships in the culinary canon. Lobster, then, became a bridge connecting watercress and caviar. The cream of watercress itself begins as a finely blended soup of cream, onion, leeks, and watercress. A bright-green purée of watercress leaves, finely strained, is added to the cream for color and flavor. "It was difficult to find the right balance of the three main ingredients," Davy says later, "but we succeeded in making something very flavorful, very light."

The humble watercress, I later discovered, played a role in French political history. In the thirteenth century, while hunting in the vicinity of Vernon, a thirsty Saint Louis was so refreshed by a fistful of local watercress that he changed that city's arms to include three fleurs-de-lis, the symbol of French royalty, and three bunches of watercress. Taillevent himself was sufficiently confident of the qualities of watercress that he served it unaccompanied, and one presumes uncooked, "to refresh the mouth" after the fourth course of a feast prepared for Charles VI and the Comte de la Marche. Taillevent's fondness for the plant did not end there. He offered only one vegetable dish in a list of recipes suitable for Lent: a purée of cress and white beets fried and then boiled in almond milk.

DuMans is an exception in his manner: some of the other cooks in Legendre's *brigade* are sanguine enough, even in the hottest press, to grin, swagger, and crack obscene jokes under their breath. At such a time, the kitchen seems less like an atelier than the lower gun deck on a ship of war, a place of shouts and fire. *"Chaud! Chaud!"* ("Hot! Hot!"), they cry in warning as they jostle between stoves and counters with steaming pots. Flames spout and crackle in the air, steaming water billows out of giant sinks, sweat runs from their faces, down their arms. At this level, at this pace, cooking seems closer to a blood sport than a craft, complete with uniforms and scars, forearms hatched with the plum-colored marks of burns weeks and months old.

Frédéric Simonin may be the purest representative of this type in the *brigade*. He is playful and ironic, and though he works as fast as any of them he appears to be the least anxious in a slam. Of all of them, Simonin seems to have the most fun. On one occasion he shows me how to make an apricot soufflé—one of two desserts (along with lemon crêpes) prepared down-stairs in the *cuisine*. As he draws the perfect, finished soufflé from the oven, he holds it out for me to admire. *"Regarde-moi ça, regarde-moi ça,"* he says, as if he had never made one before. *"C'est pas beau comme un enfant?"* ("Look at that. Isn't that as pretty as a baby?") He sets it down on the counter. *"Regarde,"* he says, and lightly dusts its toasted golden crown with powdered sugar. *"De la neige au dessus."* ("A little snow on top.")

Clogs, like the blue-and-white-checked pants, are all but ubiquitous in the kitchens of Taillevent. Though Legendre usually wears faded jeans under his apron and white jacket, his cooks and assistants wear subtle varia-tions of a uniform that has been standard in French kitchens for decades. The clogs, which appear surpris-ingly casual in the industrial and vaguely militaristic order of the working kitchen, were adopted for their comfort over long hours standing at the stoves on hard floors. French cooking clogs, whether open or closed at the heel, are often fitted with internal steel toe boxes to protect the feet from falling knives and heavy crates. I have never seen a sharp or heavy object hit the floor in my time at Taillevent, but it would take only one in a career to sell you on the steel toe. The clogs are with few exceptions white, to ensure that they are kept clean, like the double-breasted white cooking jacket worn above checked pants. The centerpiece of the chef's uniform, the white jacket is undeniably sharp. On purely superficial grounds, the jacket—really more of a heavy, pressed shirt—makes you want to cook professionally the way a set of full riding leathers makes you want to race high-performance motorcycles. Legendre rides a motorcycle to work, as it happens, and, judging from the number of helmets atop the lockers in the staff locker room upstairs, so do most of his cooks.

As any professional will tell you, cooking is often brutal work. It has been more than a decade since I last worked in an American restaurant, and I have forgotten how much a kitchen takes out of you. At the end of a full shift at Taillevent, even as an apprentice or observer, I am usually reeling with fatigue. I can say from experience that it is at the very least as tiring as laboring all day on a typical construction crew in the summer sun of a temperate climate, and usually more so. The intense heat, the pace, the close quarters, the demand for concentration, combined with long hours and relatively meager pay—it's a small wonder that burn-out and staff turnover are so prevalent in the industry on both sides of the Atlantic.

Early in my time at Taillevent, following the advice of one of the pastry cooks, I found a store that sold professional uniforms a short walk from the Gare de l'Est. I was less enamored of the white clogs and checked pants, and gave them a miss, figuring I could pass inspection in a jacket, the white kerchief worn about the neck, and the knee-length white apron. I washed and ironed the ensemble at home, and put it on before the full-length mirror. I adjusted the kerchief—most of the cooks wore the simple knot inside the collar of the jacket—and slung a folded white cloth over the apron string, on my right hip. Yes, I thought, with the satisfaction of a boy in a full-sized fire hat, that will do.

On one morning as an apprentice in the kitchen, I am awarded the unpleasant task of plucking the feathers from pigeon heads. As directed, I briefly boil the heads, holding the avian corpses over a bubbling pot. If you boil them too long, I discover, the skin cooks through and becomes tender; it is then difficult to remove the feathers without scalping the birds, revealing their walnut-sized skulls. If you boil them too briefly, the feathers resist extraction. The pigeons are served cut down the middle and laid flat, with the skulls and brains bisected and roasted with the rest of the bird. Call me a culinary lightweight, but pigeon brains in their own skulls are fairly low on my list of French delicacies, and somewhere in the vicinity of pig's-feet sausages, also on the menu, rolled in the beautiful weblike lace of their own entrails. After a time I am grateful to be transferred to another post, where I shell *langoustines* with two Japanese apprentices. Still later, I stem mushrooms and chat with Legendre across the counter of the *garde-manger*.

I ask if he feels that great chefs are more often born or made. "More often born," he says. I ask him what he considers to be the greatest danger to the chef. "Sloth," he says immediately. "The work is exhausting, and a lazy cook won't last." I ask if he has seen any differences, generally speaking, between men and women cooks. This he pauses to consider. "Women have finer palates, by and large," he says, "but they are generally less inventive. Cooking is not mathematics."

A tiny enclosed cubicle with a tinted window adjoining the kitchen serves as Legendre's office. Above his desk, partially covered by postcards and pictures, hangs a green metal street sign that reads "Gramercy Tavern." A red stuffed bear lies facedown beside the phone. Photographs and children's artwork cover the walls. A flower, each petal a different color, signed "Thomas" in a young but steady hand. A drawing of a tall, thin house with a peaked red roof and an arched door like a mouse hole. There are countless photographs of his sons at varying ages, lolling on beds, fishing in and out of boats, and pictures of Legendre himself, smiling broadly, with his family, standing beside other chefs, sitting around tables with friends. He looks so relaxed and happy in some of these photographs that he is almost unrecognizable to me; I have not seen that side of him. At the end of my time there, I arrive at the kitchen with two magnums of chilled champagne to share with the cooks, in gratitude for their time and patience. *"Vache!"* exclaims a *commis*, grinning as I set the bottles down on the counter of the *garde-manger*, and the others gather round in good cheer. I say a few words of thanks, and raise a toast to their excellence. Davy is there, and Bajolle with his staff, and I even manage to talk a few of the servers into hoisting a glass, to the joking dismay of the cooks, but Legendre doesn't bother to appear. An egg with a friend before champagne with strangers, I suppose, but it saddens me.

As I chat with Legendre over the *langoustines*, Davy

looks over receipts for the produce delivered that morning. At the service counter, two waiters carefully inspect a stack of dinner plates, turning them in the light. The plates were new six months ago, but there are already scratches in the surface, and they will be returned. On the prep counter, Simonin cuts veal kidneys into morsels, and prepares what is for me the decidedly unappetizing *ris de veau*, the white thyroid glands that grow in the calf's neck and groin. Call it an unfair prejudice, but there is something about glands that does not invite consumption. Why glands are any less appealing than muscle fiber is uncertain; I suppose it is a lack of early exposure. Most Americans grow up eating steak and ground chuck; they are habituated to muscle and find its consumption natural. Glands, on the other hand, remind us of our own glands, swollen in our throats during a cold, and, like organ meats in general for many, a step too far down the food chain. For the French, of course, or for Americans in the model of Julia Child, brain and gland and stomach and tongue are not to be abhorred but savored. They are rare specialties, far more desirable than mere steak. The negative attitude toward organs is quite new; not so very long ago, most Americans grew up eating liver and kidneys and sweetbreads, and many still do. In the 1914 edition of Fannie Farmer, there were twenty-one recipes for sweetbreads alone. In the latest edition, not a one. An editor and Francophile of my acquaintance recently told me of the first calf's brain she ate in

France some years ago. Fortunately, I heard the tale on an empty stomach. The seat of the calf's final thoughts was served intact, and "unadorned," as she put it, a pale brain entire in the middle of the plate. She assured me it was quite delicious.

At the stoves, Guibert starts the sauces. At one point he opens two wine bottles, turns them end-up over a copper pot, taps them gently together, and spirals the bottles swiftly in tight, opposing circles. The spirals create a funnel of swirling bubbles in the bottles, and the wine shoots out in a twin, foaming spray, as if under pressure. In a flash both bottles are empty. I learn a number of practical tips in the kitchens of Taillevent, and the simplest are usually the most helpful: a damp cloth or paper towel laid out under a cutting board keeps it from slipping across a counter; three small cuts in the middle of a fish skin make sure it won't contract and pull up along the edges as it cooks; a layer of plastic wrap pressed down to the level of the ingredients in a bowl eliminates air pockets and improves conservation. And so forth.

Back in the dining room, several minutes after the soup bowls have been cleared away, the escargots arrive at our table at 9:23. Served in flat soup bowls, deprived of their shells, more than a dozen of the grey-brown creatures form an islet in a sea of foaming, lemon-colored sauce speckled with minced parsley. Through that obscure process in which a previously enamored palate rewires our aesthetic sense, the creatures look not ugly but delicious. The sauce is warm, rich, and densely layered with flavor—with little doubt, it is the best sauce I've ever had.

It is a modified *sauce poulette*, a classic traditionally served over calves' or sheep's trotters, less commonly with mussels. According to Escoffier, the *sauce poulette* is essentially a *sauce allemande* (also known as the *sauce parisienne*), fortified with extra butter and reduced mushroom-cooking liquor, then sprinkled with parsley. The *sauce allemande*, says Escoffier, calls for ordinary velouté (which requires roux), white stock, mushroom-cooking liquor, egg yolks, nutmeg, lemon juice, pepper, and butter. As one can see from this example, there are sauces within sauces within sauces at the heart of French classic cuisine, and no want of butter all around. For his purposes, Legendre altered the sauce with the addition of snail stock, to bring out the flavor of the escargots. "It's just a cream sauce," Davy blithely tells me later, "finished with a little egg. The snails are slowly cooked in the oven with vegetables and a little water for an hour, an hour and a quarter. We serve the snails over a bit of sorrel cooked in butter. Since sorrel is somewhat acidic, and the snails are mild, the acidity of the sorrel helps bring out the flavors of the snails and the sauce. The sauce goes well because it's very mild, very light."

Only minutes before, *chef de partie* Olivier Limousin had prepared the snails. Spreading a dab of sautéed sorrel the size of a silver dollar in the bottom of each bowl, he strained the snails from a copper pot where they sat warm by the stove and arranged them in neat little pyramids atop the sorrel. Then he spooned out the sauce, being careful to include the foam raised by a hand-held electric blender, and finished the plates with a dash of diced fresh parsley.

The snails are tender and delicious, but I'm dismayed to discover that Erin finds the sauce too salty. To my taste, the sauce rides the line. I wonder if they may have salted the dish more heavily for our American palates, and later ask Davy. He claims that a chef never varies the seasoning for a particular guest unless requested, striving instead for flawless uniformity. The chef works from the presumably near-perfect balance of his own palate, and never wanders. Chez Panisse in Berkeley being the most celebrated exception, one of the innumerable marks of a great kitchen is its ability to produce precisely the same dish night after night, month after month, as long as it remains on the menu. The dish must be as unvarying as it is successful. In this way, haute cuisine shares something with its malformed nephew, fast food.

Entire volumes can and have been written about salt, but I will make do with a cursory glance. It derives its name from Salus, the Roman god of health, from which descends the French *salut* (and our "salute"), originally intended as a blessing on the recipient's health. The salinity of human blood is very close to that of seawater, a holdover from our days in the primordial soup, before the guppies in our family tree decided, against their better judgment, to establish a beachhead. Progressive sodium depletion leads to muscle cramps, vomiting, circulatory problems, coma, and death. While individuals suffering from severe salt deprivation have chewed dirt, the dangers of an oversalted diet are also apparent. In *Food in History,* Reay Tannahill claims that "an ounce of salt a day . . . can shorten a man's life by as much as thirty years." This might alarm my beloved mother-in-law, in most respects a paragon of moderation, who would salt an anchovy if given the chance. Thirty years lost to a saltshaker might be hard to account for, but too much sodium does lead to water retention, and has long been associated, inconclusively, with hypertension.

Prehistoric man, being almost wholly carnivorous, received an ample supply of salt in wild game. As Neolithic man began to shift the bulk of his diet from meats to vegetables and grains, his salt intake declined uncomfortably. Rather than chew dirt, he invented salt mining. Whereas the U.S. predominantly uses powdered rock salt, sea salt—called *sel marin* by the French—is widely preferred in Europe.

The average gallon of seawater (or blood) contains in suspension slightly more than a quarter-pound of salt. Waverly Root tells us that, if all the salt in all the oceans of the world was extracted and neatly scattered on the earth's landmasses, it would cover every inch of dry land to a depth of 115 feet. I wondered how much land the salt in our equally saline, collective human blood might cover, and began to make some computations. Based on a current world population of 6.1 billion, multiplied by the average human blood volume of 5 quarts, we arrive at the handy figure of 7.62 billion gallons of human blood. Dividing that sum into the oceans' total volume, however, or some 316,000,000 trillion (316,220,000,000,000,000,000) gallons, and the more dire equations that followed, quickly exceeded my ability to operate a pocket calculator. Among other problems, I began to get letters, including a lower case "e," in my numeric results. I decided to leave the oceans alone. Until we lose California, the surface area of the planet's dry land holds at 510,066,000 square kilometers. Accepting the average weight of 4 ounces of salt per gallon of human blood, we arrive at a total weight of 1.9 billion pounds for the amassed fortune of human salt. Which means that all the salt in all the blood of our fine and murderous species would not even cover Rhode Island to a depth of 7.5 feet—an improvement on Providence, perhaps, but short work for my mother-in-law and a few snowplows. Breed as we might, we're no match for the oceans in salt.

Petronius gave us our expression "not worth his salt." Roman soldiers were often paid in salt and other rations, and if not, with *salarium*, or "salt money," with which to buy it. From this Latin term we derive our "salary." Accidentally spilled salt has long been considered a harbinger of bad luck; Judas is knocking over the salt in Leonardo's *Last Supper*. We may also recall the fate of Lot's wife, turned into a pillar of salt (to the delight, no doubt, of subsequent generations of live-stock along that stretch of road) for glancing back at the destruction of Sodom. Despite this punitive association, salt was associated with Christianity and goodness from an early date. Witches and devils are purported to fear it, and be burned by it. This explains the French custom of calling a meal in which no salt is served a "witches' supper." In the Middle Ages, salt played another role in the deterrence of crime. Tannahill informs us that the decapitated heads of medieval criminals, before being set out on public display, were parboiled "with bay salt and cumin seed—that to keep them from putrefaction, and this to keep off the fowls."

On All Saints' Day, on the Isle of Man, each member of the household traditionally packed a thimble with salt and placed it facedown on a plate, in a ring. Carefully removing the thimbles, the anxious family members revealed a circle of minute salt castles. They could not have slept particularly well, for if one of the towers had collapsed by morning its builder could expect to be dead within the year. I'm sure the invention of the lazy Susan dates from this time.

The two polished silver shakers stand together on one end of our table, and there they shall remain. I would like to meet the fearless gastronome who would dare season anything that issued from that kitchen. Word of such an act would surely return to the chef, probably before the salt had landed in the sauce. "The gentleman at table four has salted his snails," the waiter might say to Legendre. Depending on the waiter, it might be said with a good deal of Schadenfreude. If the sauce is significantly off, someone in the kitchen will get his. There will be shouting, profanity, insults. Angering a chef with a known temper is like baiting a bear— plenty of fun except for the dog who gets caught. In any case, for some waiters, passing such news to the chef is its own reward. Legendre's chin might drop as he met the waiter's eyes. "Ah yes?" After a beat, with studied nonchalance, he might take the two steps to the corner of the stove, to the collection of sauces prepared and coddled by his saucier over varying degrees of low heat. He would dip a spoon into the copper pot containing the sauce in question. An omniscient, pondering taste would follow. The saucier, who works not a yard from the counter and would almost certainly have heard the remark, would be trying his best to remain unconcerned. He is Legendre's *second sous-chef,* and as such his technique is certainly beyond reproach. From such a position at Taillevent he might move to the command of a one-star French kitchen or better. He has made the sauce countless times in exactly the same way, and has tasted this very sauce within the quarter-hour. And yet, suddenly, he is unsure, like a man asked by his wife, as they enter a theater, if he locked the car, for she left her bag in the foot well. He always locks the car, compulsively, and she knows it. To park and leave his car unlocked in the exterior world would be as contrary to his body's endlessly ingrained physical memory as returning his toothbrush to its cup without banging it briskly on the sink's rim. And yet. He doubles back to check.

In all probability, Legendre's expression would relax, and he would glance back at the waiter. "Is he French?" he might ask. "American," the possible reply. Legendre would return to his position at the end of the counter. Pearls before swine. "Thank you," he would say to the waiter, in a tone so flat that the word could not possibly be misconstrued as gratitude—indeed, as anything but a dismissal of the waiter, the American, his employer, of everyone, in fact, beyond these tiled walls. He has his kitchen and a well-trained crew; for the rest, the chef could not care less.

For its part, pepper was prized in the ancient and medieval world and, like salt, was often used as payment. Alaric the Visigoth spared Rome a sacking in the year 408 thanks to a bribe that included three thousand pounds of pepper. Forty-four years later, Attila was pacified in like fashion with gifts including pepper and cinnamon. If the Huns did indeed subsist for months on the blood sucked directly from small veins in their horses' necks, you can hardly fault their decision to expand their culinary horizons in lieu of plundering a city on the wane.

Native to Malabar and Tranvancore, what we generally know as pepper grows not on a tree but on a vine that will climb, if supported, to a height of more than thirty feet. Pepper vines are commonly planted on plantations of palm, mango, or betel trees and are trained to climb them. Fresh peppercorns are green and soft and may be mashed or eaten whole. Black and white pepper begins as the same peppercorn, the seed of the *Piper nigrum*. For black pepper, the corns are picked and dried before they have completely ripened. The black color is caused by a harmless fungus on the dried skin. For white pepper, the corns are allowed to ripen to a red tint on the vine, then soaked in water to soften their skins, which are removed with the pulps. The skinless seeds are then dried. Julia Child swears by the white variety in cream sauces, disliking the speckled appearance of its darker cousin.

At 9:37, the sommelier returns to our table to check on the wine. Sensing our interest, he remains to chat. I ask him what distinguishes *grand cru* wines from their inferior brethren. The vines of a *grand cru* grow higher on the slopes than lesser vines, he explains, and their roots must dig deeper for water. Mr. Vrinat glides up to the table with a smile and listens, his hands behind his back. Although he knows all this, you have the impression that wine talk to Vrinat, however fundamental, is endlessly engaging. In certain cellars in Champagne, the sommelier continues, you can see the roots growing down the walls, some to a length of seventeen or eighteen meters. (Fifty-odd feet, it seems to me, is a long way for a plant with a trunk the diameter of a child's wrist to dig for water, especially through rocky soil. What, I wonder, did it drink on the way down?) There is a correlation, Bonnot says, between the length of the roots and the complexity of the resulting wine. *"Le plus la vigne souffre,"* he concludes, with that marvelous French capacity to extract an elegantly defeatist philosophy of art and life from the culturally super-specific, *"le meilleur le vin."* ("The more the vine suffers, the better the wine.")

The empty escargot bowls—my own buffed with bread morsels to an immaculate shine—are soon cleared. At 9:47, the captain serves our third appetizer, the *mousseline d'oeufs.* In the middle of each plate is a ring of scrambled egg topped with a sprig of parsley. Surrounding the egg are morels and spears of young asparagus in a pale sauce. *Chef de partie* Jérôme Tixier prepared our *mousseline,* with the help of *commis* David Bizet. Tixier is one of the few cooks in the kitchen to wear black clogs. He cooked the egg until creamy, and poured it into a low steel ring in the middle of the empty plate; as it began to cool, it assumed the ring's shape, retaining it when the ring, like a billiard rack, was carefully lifted up and away.

When Tixier cracks eggs at Taillevent, he raps them on a flat surface—never on an edge, which can push minute fragments of shell into the egg. At the *entremets,* he is responsible for eggs, soups, mushrooms, asparagus, carrots, beans, and other warm vegetables. When he has steamed or boiled green vegetables, he dunks them in cold water for two to three minutes—never longer—to arrest the cooking process and preserve flavor. Behind him is a tray of herbs and spices, including diced chives, shallots, chervil, and a bowl of mixed salt and pepper. To prepare the shallots, he dices them finely, rinses them in a bath of cold water to remove the bitterness, and wrings them out in a cloth. The shallots will keep for two days. Tixier is cheerful and quick. During a service, by necessity, he appears to work as fast as or faster than anyone in the kitchen. *"Entremets,"* he later tells me, in the midst of a frenzied *coup de feu,* "is the hottest station in the kitchen, in every sense of the term." Red-faced, gleaming with sweat, he flits his hands back and forth from pan to plate to pot in a blur of sustained activity. This speed is all the more extraordinary when I realize that his movements are not slapdash: he is performing one extremely precise motion after another.

"The association between morels and asparagus is classic," Davy later tells me, "but we tried to put them with other things, and with eggs they marry very well. It was Philippe's idea. There are certain things we try always to have on the menu. We're obliged to have eggs, beef, and veal, among other things. So we looked for something that might go with egg. It wasn't easy, because egg is mild but distinct. There aren't many things that go well with it."

For the sauce, the cooks sauté the morels in butter with shallots until they release all their water. Then they add a little cream, cook it gently for twenty minutes, and blend it thoroughly. They boil and butter the asparagus.

Though the sauce is a bit too salty for both of us, and the egg, to our taste, is too bland, the asparagus are extraordinary, and the morels are the best mushrooms I've ever had. The plates are cleared at 10:06, and a *chef de rang* sweeps the table with a silver brush.

La Pause

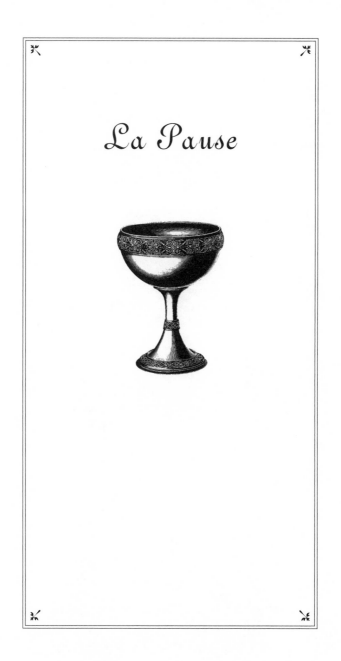

At 10:10, the captain reappears and sets two frosted glass goblets before us—the kind of vessels in which ice-cream sundaes are often served. "To mark the pause," he says. There is something pink and cold at the bottom of each goblet—a ball of sorbet, by appearance, not quite the size of a golf ball, ridged with spirals as if pressed through a serrated pastry tip in slow rotation.

On a weekday afternoon some weeks before, at the suggestion of Gilles Bajolle, I met with retired *homme d'affaires* and amateur cook François Cochet at a café on the corner of the rue Balzac. Cochet is a passionate gourmand and self-taught expert on the subject of French gastronomy. Born in Fontainebleau, a resident of Paris since 1950, he went to business school with Jean-Claude Vrinat, and in 1960 co-founded a printing company. Since his retirement, he has studied as an apprentice in the greatest kitchens of France, including those of Taillevent, Robuchon, and Trois Gros.

"Cooking is never an invention," Cochet told me. "It is always an evolution. I've never liked the chefs who are overly inventive. It's a bit like painting: after the impressionists we had the cubists and the expressionists, and now *on fait n'importe quoi*. You've seen that English painter who sold the brains and entrails of animals for enormous sums? One such piece sold for 150,000 pounds. It's excessive, but that's the fashion. Three hundred thousand dollars. It's the same in music. Mozart wrote popular operas; now the popular does not exist in serious music. In cooking nowadays, there are chefs who mix things like coffee with *ris de veau*."

We spoke of the changes in French cooking over the last fifty years.

"When you read the cookbooks from before the war," he said, "you realize that at that time there were *fonds* sauces, where you simmered the bones and meat in water over many hours. That extracted the juices, and very strong flavors. Now that's finished. We cook in somewhat the same manner, but only just so. We don't cook as long, and now we make *jus*. Before the war we used an enormous amount of flour; almost all the sauces had flour to thicken them. We used a great deal of crème fraîche. Now cooking has become lighter, but the tastes are not, in fact, that different. I observed a few things *chez* Robuchon. He is someone with a sense of invention, but his inventions are more or less successful.

"In my opinion, Philippe is truly one of the best. To be sure, he's in a traditional restaurant. Taillevent is very classical, very BCBG *(bon chic bon genre)*. During the day it is business lunches, people who have been *très bien élevés*. There is no noise. So the cooking must remain reasonable, not shocking, not inventive. Classical cuisine, taken to the highest level. It is excellent, certainly. But in my opinion Vrinat will have problems.

"Now, Alain [Davy] is not ambitious, but he too is a great cook. He is happy to be a *sous-chef,* but he is a great cook. One quality, which for me is very important, is that at Taillevent there is very little variation in the flavors of a dish over time. Philippe is very skilled in this respect, and it is a great quality in a restaurant: you have a dish, and if you come back two weeks later and have it again it will taste the same. At Taillevent, they are very precise.

"Philippe is an extremely dynamic young man. Always under pressure, and that's terribly exhausting. The problem for a cook like Philippe is that he's always in his kitchen. He doesn't have much time to look around him, to see how other people are doing things. He's also a bit imprisoned by the menu, and if there is one awful thing in the life of the professional cook, a horrible thing, it's that you always have to do the same dish. You repeat, you repeat, you repeat. Every day the same gestures, the same tasks. Philippe is pinned down by his work. It's an enormous job. Eight-thirty in the morning until midnight, with two free hours in the afternoon. That's one of the big problems for all chefs, generally speaking. Nearly all the chefs I've seen pay little or no attention to what their peers are doing. It doesn't interest them. It's a sort of pride. Philippe is not really this way—he's very open—but he doesn't get out."

I asked Cochet what he believes is required to produce a chef of Legendre's caliber.

"On the one hand, there is talent, a gift. At the level

of the palate, and in the transmission, if you will, between the palate and the creative mind. On the other, the best chefs know through their training and experience that this and that ingredient, for example, could never work together.

"Philippe can be difficult in the kitchen. Nearly all chefs are difficult. But he is quick to anger; very *soupe au lait*." Cochet mimicked milk boiling up and out of a hot pan. "The main problem for Philippe at Taillevent is that he doesn't get along with his employer. Either they're indifferent, or they're not talking, or they're yelling back and forth. There are no meetings to say, 'Okay, Philippe, you've done well.' Mr. Vrinat does not know how to congratulate, because he is terribly hard on himself. He's never satisfied. And he doesn't realize that there are times when you have to tell people they've done a good job. Instead, he'll say things like, 'What you have done does not even merit a single Michelin star.' That sort of remark."

Nonetheless, I observed, the kitchen seems to work very well.

"It's true that Taillevent is one of the restaurants in France that works best," said Cochet. "I speak of the great restaurants. I assure you, you must see what goes on in many restaurants. The number of people who can pay a thousand francs per person is not very great. In general, at lunch, it is ninety-eight percent businessmen. In the evening, a few French, and wealthy foreigners. But often the foreigners are there on business. A group from Coca-Cola that comes to Paris and reserves three or four suites—they're not paying their own way. So the restaurants at the highest level in France are extremely endangered, because they're too expensive. When I say 'too expensive' I don't mean that the prices are too high relative to what they offer, but that they are too high relative to what most people can pay. The problem is that there are many restaurants that are very expensive and not very good, in the quality of their products and in their preparation. The worst is Loiseau in Saulieu. What prices, and it was nothing, nothing, *mauvais*. I had a little piece of beef for three hundred and fifty francs. The bill was twelve hundred francs per person for nothing, *pour des trucs nuls!* Likewise at Pierre Gagnaire, on the rue Balzac. The other day I thought about the number of restaurants I know in France. An enormous number. And, frankly, Taillevent is certainly one of the restaurants that I prefer.

"The chef who was there before Philippe was very good, but a bit old-fashioned," he said. "A bit too much in the old style. He was not very creative. Philippe is very inventive, and at the same time he remains very classical, because his employer quite rightly insists upon it.

"Now, Gilles, I can tell you, is a genius of pastry. Philippe is a very, very great cook, but Gilles is a genius. The simplest dough he makes is just extraordinary. To begin with, he has improved the fundamentals, the basics. His *mille-feuille*—it's astounding. The puff pastry is magnificent. It melts in the mouth. It's too bad that this young man cannot express himself. The main problem at Taillevent is that the chef and the pastry chef are not acknowledged. There is *one* owner. Taillevent is Mr. Vrinat. The rest, who knows?

"Of all the chefs I've worked with as a kind of visiting apprentice, I've surely learned the most from Philippe. There are famous restaurants, here and in the provinces, where I was very disappointed by what I saw in the kitchens. I once visited Robuchon. It was very difficult. The discipline was a horror. They worked in a deathly silence. He's a *tyrant*, Robuchon. A fabulous professional, but a tyrant. And I have seen mistakes in his restaurant. Grave mistakes. I took my children to dinner there; my daughter had a dish of prawns and ravioli, and it was insufficiently cooked. We said nothing; we knew that if we mentioned it someone would kill himself in the kitchen."

I asked Cochet what he considered to be the greatest danger for a professional chef.

"Pride," he answered. "When there are successes in this industry, you often see manifestations of enormous pride. Not in everyone, but that's the greatest danger. The second great danger is the routine. Because it's very exhausting, very difficult."

I asked about the predominance of male chefs in the industry, especially in France.

"It's a man's trade—why? Perhaps because it's hard physical work, perhaps because the men are macho and don't want women in their kitchens. In the large bourgeois families of the nineteenth century,

there were only women in the kitchens; they were
employees, cooks. The chefs were with the aristocratic
families. Escoffier worked for the *duc de je ne sais
quoi,* who had twenty-five guests for dinner every day.
Fine. But it's a terribly macho milieu, and now in
France there is one female *chef de cuisine*— one. I speak
of the *grands restaurants.* Madame Arabian, who was
at Ledoyen. There are a few women in the industry,
but very few. Before the war there was a woman in
Lyon who was a great cook. In any case, women have
a greater reputation for traditional cuisine, for refined
home cooking."

I asked him what he thought of Legendre's opinion
on the differences between men and women cooks.

"I don't agree," he said. "To begin with, the doors of
the great kitchens are closed to women. I can't think of
any reason why a woman would not be as inventive as a
man. I'm not a feminist, but objectively speaking. It's
true that in certain disciplines, like music, female com-
posers are very rare. There are practically no women
conductors. I think it's habit, a tradition of male predominance. Ask your wife what she thinks.

"For a chef new ideas come more or less by chance.
It's very rare that a chef will say to himself, 'Here I am
in front of the stove, now what shall I create?' No. Ideas
come from time to time, he writes them down, he tries
them. The chef, sadly, makes a product for immediate
consumption that disappears. An artist can make something for a museum, something that remains, but the
chef starts over twice a day."

I asked him about the emotional impulse that drives a chef, the desire to nourish or give pleasure.

"When I cook, I too have that desire. But for a professional chef, thanks to the repetition, that rarely exists. If Philippe invites a few good friends over and prepares a meal, he will certainly feel those emotions. Otherwise, it's *boulot, boulot, boulot* [work, work, work]. Repetition, let me repeat, is a terrible thing. Terrible. The problem for a chef during a service is above all the arrival of the clients. If all the clients arrive at the same time, it's a catastrophe. Because for twenty-five or thirty people there will be ten or twelve different dishes, and they must all be prepared and delivered at the same time. This is the chef's nightmare. You see that we are already very far from those fine and generous emotions. Between that generosity—the happiness that one would like to give to others—and the profession, lies a world. When there are clients, and they say the food is very good, of course the cooks will be happy, because that is their goal. But during the service, they're not thinking about that at all. In any case, I've never met a chef of great reflection.

"The great chefs are often very warm, but I've never met a chef who fascinated me, if you will, through his intelligence, through his vision of the world. I won't say they're materialists, because that's not the word, but I've never heard a chef speak of anything other than cooking. *Ou alors de cul* [or about ass].

"Gilles is not at all like that, but Gilles is a case apart. Gilles is very, very interested in things, and he has researched a great deal. When he travels, he tries to learn. He's very curious. Pastry cooks are a bit different from cooks, but Gilles is truly a case apart. He's a very sharp young man. But as I said earlier, most cooks are people without any intellectual formation. Many do not know how to spell. They're incapable of writing a letter. Incapable of writing a text: to announce the subject of their letter, to develop it, and to conclude. It's just terrible.

"Among the great restaurants nowadays there are Robuchon and Taillevent; perhaps Senderens at Lucas Carton. What is also very important is the quality of the clients. At Taillevent the clientele is extraordinary. Everyone who counts, I would say, in business at a very high level, goes to Taillevent for lunch, because they feel comfortable there. At Taillevent there is a sort of magical ambience that is doubtless due to the décor and to the quality of the staff. Taillevent is something other than a restaurant. It is a place blessed by the gods. When you're at Taillevent, you arrive, you sit down, you're in a completely protected world. People take care of you without troubling you. You feel protected, as a child feels protected by his parents. You're in a kind of bliss.

"It's true that a dinner is better than a lunch. When you're going to Taillevent, eight hours before, you begin to look forward to it. That is happiness. And in the evening it's all very lovely. When it's dark, at eight o'clock, you're not shocked by the artificial light. But at lunchtime it's a bit somber. There are no windows. It's a bit gloomy at midday.

"One should arrive as early as possible. Seven-forty-five or eight o'clock. That is the ideal time, because people who come to eat at ten in the evening have not prepared their palates. They're too hungry, because they haven't eaten, or they ate something earlier in the evening, or they've been drinking. You must have a good clean palate.

"The perfect client, when he is happy and content, asks the *maître d'hôtel* to tell the kitchen. But often the servers don't pass the word, because they and the cooks are not the best of friends. Some get along very well with the kitchen, but many don't. Some of them will say, 'It's taking too long,' or 'The client is unhappy,' but never 'The client is content.' You must understand that the kitchen is a microcosm. You have all the sentiments of the world: familiarity, hatred, love—perhaps not love—but it's a closed world.

"Cooking, for me, is truly the notion of happiness—not pleasure, not the pleasure of the palate, but to make a pasta for good friends, to invite people over. It is a means of knowing people better, of entering into a certain intimacy. When I have guests, they know in advance that I will be doing something particularly for them, and I know that they will look forward to it. It is the notion of *fête,* of conviviality. I should say that I have never had a dinner party that involved the slightest bit of vulgarity. Never. When I make a meal, my manner encourages no one in that direction. Because I don't like that at all."

I try to imagine what kind of vulgarity he is referring to, and I suppose he means drunkenness, bawdy innuendo, groping in the coatroom. But the French sense of propriety is so different from our own that I cannot be sure. In some ways the French are infinitely more proper and discreet than we are; in other ways they're more French. For all I know, a vulgar guest in France is one who drops a name or brags of a recently acquired property, whereas one who palms the hostess in the kitchen is merely considered an enthusiast.

The pink substance in our goblets is indeed sorbet, after a fashion, and the first handiwork—beside the gougères—of Gilles Bajolle. It is a ball of lightly sweetened frozen champagne, and when Erin tastes it she closes her eyes. The champagne melts and sparkles on the tongue. After another taste she leans over and declares, "This is the best thing so far."

Le Plat

While we are finishing our sorbet, Legendre calls for the lobster and the sea bream amidst a stream of other courses. "Chef!" confirms Romain Marzet, a twenty-four-year-old *chef de partie*, who prepares the fish for cooking. Marzet pulls a large fillet of bream from a covered tray in a refrigerator beneath the fish-preparation counter. The gilthead bream is perhaps the most highly prized of the sea-bream family, a group that includes the porgy, the scup, and the Atlantic sheepshead. The flesh is white and flaky and very delicate in flavor. Marzet prepared the fillets earlier in the day from a whole fish delivered on ice that morning. No fish served at Taillevent has been out of the water more than two days.

Born in Sens, Burgundy, Marzet completed a *bac* in economics before turning to cooking. He finds Taillevent much better organized and much more harmonious than other kitchens of his experience, its food notably, and relatedly, superior. He attributes this to Legendre. "A kitchen's ambience," he says, "comes from the chef."

Marzet lays the fillet of bream on a plate and hands it to Vincent Dautry, a *demi-chef de partie* who helps work the stoves. There are two *chefs de partie* in the fish department on this particular evening, Frédéric

Simonin and Lionel Durand. All three have a hand in the cooking. Between them, working on a number of dishes at once, they sauté the *daurade* in olive oil, drain it briefly on a white cloth, and plate it, skin up, over sautéed tomatoes and basil. The glittering black-and-silver-scaled skin of the *daurade* is one of the most beautiful things I will see in this kitchen. The *daurade*'s preparation could hardly be simpler, a variation on a classic Mediterranean recipe employed for centuries. The important thing, Davy later tells me, is to cook the fish *à point*, and to use an olive oil that is flavorful without being overpowering. "You need to respect the balance of flavors," he says. "There are excellent oils, but some of them are very potent, and when you cook with them you taste nothing but olive oil."

Marzet now passes the lobster meat—a tail, cut in slices in its green-black carapace, and a large claw—to Dautry. The lobster goes into a pan on the stove and in moments is spattering in oil.

In Crete, the winter before we were married, my wife and I came across a small olive-oil factory beside a narrow road south of Chania. We had been passing olive groves for days, women beating the trees while the olives rained down upon cloths stretched beneath them. We had rented a car, to traverse the distances between eastern and western Crete, and we parked at the sight of this small, bustling factory shimmering in a haze of olive oil. The air around it was dense with the smell, and when we stepped through the open door the scent became so potent that you could taste it in the air on your tongue. Over the din of the machines, we asked one of the workers if we could buy some fresh oil, and watch for a while as they pressed it. Certainly, he said, and gave us a tour. An elderly woman appeared from a side room and offered us two cups of Turkish coffee. Half a dozen men worked a chain of machines in a space no bigger than a mechanic's garage. Delivered by donkey or pickup truck, the olives came in by the bagful through the back door and into a floor well, whence they were aspirated into a machine that stripped away most of the leaves. The olives were washed in another machine, then ground with the pits into a pulp. Next the pulp was sterilized through the addition of water heated by a furnace fueled by olive pits. An old Cretan stood before the furnace with a shovel, feeding the dried pits to the fire. The pulp was spun in a centrifuge, to separate the oil from the pits and water. Two more centrifuges followed, to separate the water further, before the oil, a deep, smoky green, poured into huge vats. Another man filled barrels from the vats with a nozzle that resembled a gas pump. Offering us bread, our guide encouraged us to dip it into an open container of fresh oil. This oil, he said, had been in olives on the tree that morning.

I can scarcely express the potency of that first taste. It coated the mouth and throat like resin. This was not the oil for Taillevent. This was an oil that would obliterate the flavors of nearly anything it touched. It was the blood of Crete; in it you could taste the trees and roots and rocks of the surrounding hills. It held the vital

current of a living thing. Our host filled our tall, empty
water bottle to the brim with oil, and refused payment
with a wave of his hand. We thanked him and drove
north to Chania, the bottle between us, the car's interior
rich with its scent.

Last winter, Legendre encountered a dish of meat
and chestnuts at another restaurant. He wondered how
chestnut might work with seafood, and tried it unsuc-
cessfully with various fish. Then he tried it with *langoustine;* this was better, but he found the *langoustine*
too strong. He arrived finally at the present combination, where the subtle flavors of the lobster do not
overpower the chestnut. No French cook, to his knowledge, has ever before combined nuts and shellfish in a
single dish.

Chestnut trees can grow to a great age. A chestnut
planted near the foot of Sicily's Mount Etna by Romans
in the time of the Republic grew to an age of more than
two thousand years. Some sources date the tree at a
mere millennium, but even at that it was widely considered to be the oldest tree in Europe. Never ceasing in its
production of nuts, this so-called Chestnut of a Hundred Horses attained a girth of 204 feet before its
demise in an 1850 eruption.

The common European chestnut produces two varieties: the rarer, sweeter *marron,* and the *châtaigne,* as
they are called in France. The bur of a *châtaigne* carries
two or three nuts to a *marron*'s one. The *marron* is most

commonly known to us in its candied form, *marrons glacés*, a confection that appears in French homes around Christmas and might be considered too sweet even by those habituated to eating sugar cubes out of the box. I find them almost inedible, but feel quite different about roasted *châtaignes*, found in winter in cities throughout Europe, smoking in black pans, on street corners and outside metro stops. Middle-aged Eastern European men with soot-black hands, threadbare coats, and unraveling wool caps scoop the split mahogany shells piping hot into cones of newsprint. Perhaps it is the heat of their fires and the sweet burning smell of the chestnuts, or perhaps it is their brisk business, but the chestnut sellers of Paris, as a group, have always struck me as more cheerful and lively than their neighbors: the crêpe mongers in their cramped, illuminated booths, or the stone-faced kiosk operators, grudgingly selling magazines and *Officiels des Spectacles*. I like the cones of newspaper as much as I like the chestnuts. One can be driven to despair by the packaging in any American chain grocery or toy store—the wasteful and misleading size of the containers, the garish and unnatural colors, the hyperbolic, adolescent copy written in cold blood by urban adults, many of them with advanced degrees in English—"Mega Monster Cheese Balls Just Got Bigger! Whoah!" To the same degree, one feels restored by a practical, unfussy, and recycled packaging that does its second job perfectly and without fanfare. Today's news, tomorrow's chestnut wrapper.

There is a mild irony in the presence of chestnut in a

dish at Taillevent, because the *châtaigne* has long been associated with hard times. Before the potato became common in France, and for some time after, chestnuts were the staple food among the poor. Whereas the most austere diet among Anglophones might be described as bread and water, the French equivalent is *l'eau et la châtaigne*—water and chestnuts. Pairing lobster with chestnuts, then, is a bit like serving caviar with potato cakes. Which wouldn't be bad, come to think of it.

Durand steams a bit of chopped carrot and celery, adds butter and cèpe mushrooms, and then the cooked chestnuts, mixing them together over the flame. He plucks the sautéed lobster pieces out of the pan with a pair of tongs and briefly drains them on a white cloth. Using shears, he clips the shells from around the disks of tail meat, plates the lobster with the chestnuts, and dusts them with a pinch of salt and pepper. Simonin, meanwhile, has whipped a creamy, golden sauce in a metal tin, raising a head of foam with a hand-blender. Now he spoons it generously over the dish, allowing it to pool beneath the froth.

To prepare the sauce, Davy later tells me, the chestnuts are cooked in a chicken stock or other light stock. The saucier reduces a second stock, made of lobster carcasses and finely chopped carrots, leeks, celery, and garlic, and mixes it with the first. He then further reduces the sauce and adds more butter.

Davy is the most affable and easygoing cook in the kitchen. He says little during a service, but is quick to smile. It is impossible to imagine him angry. Whereas

Legendre seems brooding and troubled, Davy is uncomplicated and at ease. On one occasion, while Davy diced black truffles, a *commis* bumped him with a tray. A quarter-cup of the minute cubes fell to the tiled floor. The *commis* was abashed, but Davy gave him only the vaguest frown. From Davy this seemed a devastating reprimand. As a young *commis* I would much rather face the full, bellowing wrath of Legendre, or a derisive sneer from his saucier, than a shadow of disapproval from Davy. He bent down, collected the fallen truffle into a fine strainer, and lowered it into a bowl of clean water. He jiggled the strainer, and the grains of truffle danced gently. "The dust," he explained, "rises and floats on the surface." Then he boiled the truffle and drained it again. When it was perfectly clean, he returned the truffle to the cutting board. Not even at Taillevent will they waste truffle that costs them forty-four hundred francs, or more than seven hundred dollars, a kilogram. "Have you ever tasted raw truffle?" he asked me. I hadn't, and he handed me a shaving, two inches long. It was a deep, shiny black and textured like an elephant-skin boot, firm under the teeth, and it tasted less like a mushroom than like a pungent piece of bark or root. It had the flavor of something that had grown between the roots of an oak tree, deep in the black earth, under leaves.

Davy was born on the first of the year in 1959, in a tiny country village near Angers, on the Loire. The eldest of three, he grew up on a grain-and-dairy farm. Though neither of his parents was an avid cook, he became interested in cooking as a child, and decided at twelve that he would enter the profession. At fourteen he went to trade school, finishing with a *bac technic* at seventeen. Early in his career, he spent two years cooking at Boccaccio's in Los Angeles. As a cook in California, he said, one could find rare and wonderful ingredients, but the customers were generally unwilling to pay the higher prices such ingredients demanded. Eventually, he ended up at the restaurant Balzac in Paris, where he met Legendre. Twelve years ago, Legendre hired Davy to be his second at Taillevent.

Three days after our meal, between shifts, I meet with Davy in the refectory. I ask him if there are any specific ethics in the kitchen.

"There are general rules," he says. "In the history of cooking, an ethic has arisen naturally from the fact that if you want to produce something of a certain quality you must work a certain way. You must follow certain guidelines. There may be a kind of moral code transmitted from master to student. But there is nothing written."

"Do you find that there is a spiritual element to cooking?" I ask.

"No. I think that people who begin to confuse cooking with spirituality are taking themselves too seriously." He laughs. "You must certainly love what you're doing. If you don't love it, you won't be doing it for long. You have to take other things seriously. But never yourself."

"Do you think it's similarly dangerous to think of cooking as an art?"

"Yes. The moment you consider yourself an artist, you'll no longer be as creative in the work at hand."

"So perhaps it's better to think of it as closer to making a good chair or table?"

"Yes, that may be closer. One can certainly take satisfaction in one's work, but something spiritual? I think not. Sincerely not. I think you have to remain much simpler than that. Cooking is a pretext, a means of finding or preserving certain social and familial values. It is a means, not an end. It is always nice to find oneself around a good table, and that is one way of being close to people. But the food on the table cannot be the focus."

"But, as in the case of the martial arts, for example," I say, "the mere practice of something, as a path, can have an arguably spiritual effect on the practitioner, even if he refuses to call it that. Can it not?"

"I think that any line of work can be seen that way," he says. "When you cook, you must consecrate yourself in exactly the same way that you must in the martial arts, or in becoming a priest, or anything else. When you devote yourself to a craft, of course you will be on a kind of path."

"How is cooking an intellectual experience? Is it more creative or more mathematical?"

"I would say it's a bit of both. To arrive at the desired result, as in mathematics, you need to know the fundamentals. There are ingredients you can combine, and others you can't. You cannot evolve as a cook without these fundamentals—what we call *la cuisine classique*. Beyond that, you need to know how to adapt a dish to your own taste, to the taste of those around you. And also to the taste of the moment, because cooking is also a matter of *la mode*. You need both."

"Do you find that some chefs are stronger in one aspect than in another?"

"Of course. There are some who have a kind of genius for one side."

"Like Philippe?"

"No, I would say he is well balanced between the two."

"What is the state of mind necessary to cook well?"

"I think that if you're happy, if you're *bien dans la tête*, that will be felt in your cooking. And if you're not, if you're tense or unhappy, that too will be felt. You have to keep things simple, respect others, and respect the products. It's very hard to truly respect the products, but it's no less difficult to respect the people we're working with, especially in such an atmosphere. Sometimes, in the middle of a service, someone won't do something the way I want it done. I'll want to jump on the cook who did it, bawl him out, insult him. But I know that afterward, correctly, I would feel sick. I'd regret it. So that's it. You must learn how to live with others."

Thanks largely to hostilities with Vrinat, Legendre and Davy will move to the Hôtel George V in the fall.

Legendre never spoke of it in my presence, but there were hushed intimations in the restaurant. The formal announcement, when it came during my apprenticeship, was treated in *Le Figaro* like a major political coup. Davy now tells me that the vast majority of their *brigade* will follow them to the George V in September. He finds this reassuring, indicating as it does that the *brigade* gets along well, does not feel overly disciplined, and finds the work sufficiently rewarding. "We have created a solid group," he says. "It's good to see."

"Are there dishes on the menu that you yourself have developed?" I ask him.

"Not really, because when Philippe comes up with recipes they always come from an assembly of ideas. Someone suggests an idea, and then another idea, perhaps very far in advance, but they wind their way along, and eventually these ideas appear in a dish. In any case, it's very hard to have a menu with one idea from one person, another idea from another, and so on. The menu must have a certain coherence. So, even though different ideas, from one cook or another, will influence it, the dish is always reworked and adapted to fit in the spirit of the menu."

"So it's very common for you and Philippe to discuss ideas?"

"Every day."

"Have there been dishes that you and Philippe have created together that you think work exceptionally well?"

"No, I wouldn't see it that way. I wouldn't say that

something came from me, or from me and Philippe, because it comes from all of us."

"So the *chefs de partie* are equally involved?"

"Yes, in their own way. It's like a machine. Each of us is a working part, smaller or larger, but all necessary. If the people were different, the machine would be different, and so would the result. So it's very hard to claim something as one's own."

"Were you ever interested in pastry?"

"No. I don't know why. In fact, in the beginning I didn't have a strong preference for one or the other, but it's hard to do both. They're two different métiers, and you do one or the other. I would say that pastry seemed to me somehow less interesting. There is much more to do in the savory side of cooking than in pastry, I think."

"What were your pastimes as a child?"

"I had very few, because most of the time I was working on the farm, with my father. This was on the weekends, when I came home from school."

"Was it difficult work?"

"Oh, I always loved it. If cooking hadn't worked out, I imagine I'd still be on a farm."

"Do you have any experience in the arts or music?"

"I like music a great deal. I particularly like working with my hands around the house, fixing things, working with wood. I've tried a little painting. When I was younger, and had the time, I loved building models— boats, cars."

"As a cook, is it difficult to put so much time into work that vanishes so quickly?"

"When you make a dish, you're not going to put it under glass and keep it there. You make it for people to enjoy. It takes two hours to prepare, and five minutes to eat, but there it is."

"That must train one in the practice of letting go."

"Oh yes. It's very ephemeral. Completely. You can't see it as an architect sees his tower, a monument that may last centuries. That's the beauty of cooking as well. Each time, we start everything over."

I ask Davy about the difference between cooking professionally and cooking for friends and family.

"It's completely different," he says. "When you're at home, there is no constraint. You can take two days to make a meal if you want to. At the restaurant, every-thing must be ready the moment the client arrives, and there are other constraints—constraints of money, of time. At home, if the chicken isn't cooked when your friends arrive, no problem. You can ask them to wait a little while. When you serve friends, you can also serve them whatever you like. At the restaurant, you prepare what is ordered. You're obliged to maintain a certain style, to keep a certain dish on the menu, because you must have a range of merchandise to satisfy all clients. Even if you only like to cook fish, we don't work in a restaurant that serves only fish. So there are always constraints."

"Is it hard for you to never talk with the clients?"

"It's true that it's not easy to work all day in the kitchen, behind a wall. We don't know how people are responding. On the other hand, even when you do have contact with them, it's hard to know what they're thinking. It's always very superficial. Unless you have known them a long time, it's hard to know if people are sincere. When you have a chef who goes into the dining room, people will say, 'Yes, everything is wonderful,' or 'No, it isn't,' and it's hard to know when they're being sincere."

"But you must have criticism."

"Yes, it's always good to have criticism. Because there are critics, we can improve, and some of them are sincere. But it's always hard to know who is sincere and who is not. Some will tell you, 'It's excellent,' because you are standing in front of them and they don't want to offend you. And there are others, because they want to impress their girlfriends, who will tell you, 'This is *merde*.' You do get better at knowing whom to believe. And usually when people don't like something they'll tell you why. That can be constructive. Then you can reflect on it, and know if you've made a mistake."

I observe that this must happen very rarely at Taillevent.

"It happens," he says. "When you do something like this, you can't please everyone. And here in some ways it is more difficult: when you ask people to spend a thousand francs for a meal, they naturally expect something irreproachable. And yet, when you serve a hundred and ten people a night, in a period of two hours, there is no way that everyone can be served in the same way."

I ask him what he eats at home.

"Breakfast is usually a bit of bread and jam with a cup of tea," he says. "Lunch at home is often a salad, or a grill of some kind, or perhaps a roast chicken. For dinner, we go out, or make a pizza at home, things like that. Generally something very simple."

"Like everyone," I say.

"Why not? Do I look any different from the next guy? I'll tell you, when a chef says, 'Oh yes, at home I make my special this or that, my fancy lobster something or other . . .'" Davy produces a Bronx cheer. "No. That's strictly for image."

"When I get home after cooking all day, *j'en ai mars.*" (I've had it.) He smiles. "I want to do something else."

When Davy does cook at home, he dabbles in Italian, Thai, Chinese. Much depends on his guests, and on what he describes as *"le murmure du moment."* At home, he says, he rarely tries to re-create a dish from Taillevent. For one thing, they're often too complicated to do easily in a home kitchen. "I love Asiatic vegetable dishes. I'm going into a much more vegetarian period, I would say. I eat less and less meat. I enjoy it less and less."

I find this a minor consolation, for I have been feeling like an aberration of nature during staff meals when I decline the meat. Legendre in particular seems to consider my disinclination profoundly suspect, although he does not comment. I imagine he believes that anyone who abstains from red meat and claims an interest in French cooking is either posturing or terribly misguided, like a Catholic who professes faith in everything but Jesus and the Saints. "Well, Father, I do like Mary a lot. And God. There's always God."

"What are the other important qualities in a chef?" I ask Davy.

"His rigor, and his generosity. Those are the two engines."

"Is it very competitive to get a job here, to enter as a *commis*?"

"No, no. In any case, there is less and less demand for these kinds of jobs, because there are fewer and fewer people who want to spend twelve or fourteen hours a day in a kitchen. Anyone can come here and work."

"Anyone at all?"

"Anyone, as long as he is professional and prepared to work hard."

When the two fish dishes are ready, Dautry sets the two plates on a tray before Legendre. The chef eyes them neutrally, polishes their rims with his cloth, and covers them with steel covers. A serving *commis* floats the tray out to the dining room.

At 10:27, the goblets cleared away, the captain serves the main course. Erin receives the lobster; I am given the *daurade*. After a few bites we share, nudging our plates closer to prevent a reach. The *daurade* is nicely cooked but in context mild and unremarkable, its simple Mediterranean treatment too thin and understated after the layered, potent flavors of the creamed and buttered sauces of the appetizers.

The lobster, on the other hand, is dumbfounding. It is perfect. Though not a habitué of three-star restaurants, I have eaten my share of good food in homes and in restaurants, some hidden, some renowned. In my experience, if there is anything I have ever eaten that could be called a work of genius, this is it.

I grew up with the Maine lobster, and knew nothing of the California spiny lobster until I went out west to go to school. These lack the big claws of their Eastern cousins, but their carapaces are covered with hard spikes to discourage those predators unequipped with neoprene gloves. Charter boats running out of Santa Barbara and other towns along the southern-California coast take divers for overnight trips to the Channel Islands. There, in depths generally ranging from sixty to eighty feet, scuba divers capture lobsters by hand. I made several such trips, and in one case I more than paid for the adventure by keeping the biggest catch for myself and selling seven or eight others by the pound, perhaps illegally, to a restaurant beneath my apartment. None of them was less than four or five pounds, but the chef wanted to stretch them, so he made a bisque. After one such trip, I arranged to prepare a nine-pound lobster for my girlfriend of the time and a pair of friends. We were trying to match a friend of mine with a friend of hers, and a giant lobster seemed like a suitable ice-breaker. I felt confident my friend would take to the woman in question; she was an English major, tall and pretty and redheaded, and rode a black motorcycle. My girlfriend and I had a row at the last minute, however, and she and her friend stood us up. My friend was stoic but disappointed when the women failed to appear; it cheered him considerably when I told him we'd eat the entire nine-pound lobster ourselves. And so we did, over a chess game, and drank all the wine. The apartment overlooked Telegraph Avenue in Berkeley, at the corner of Haight Street, in sight of People's Park. It so happened that on that very afternoon a large crowd of students and the homeless had gathered to protest the university's recent forcible eviction of some portion of their number from an empty but condemned building down the street. They had been squatting, and the university feared a fire. It was a huge crowd, in fact, and the riot police turned out in rank and file, with helmets, truncheons, and Plexiglas shields. We took our lobster and a bottle of wine and went up onto the roof to observe. One of the mob's leaders had a megaphone. He stood on an upended trash can and slung epithets at the police, the university, and the government, while the police formed a square and looked hot and unhappy. Stones and bottles soon came into play, rattling and thudding against the shields, and eventually the police made a halfhearted rush. The crowd dissolved like a vapor before them, and only a few well-aimed swings of the truncheons hit their marks. We were quite drunk by this point, and stuffed with lobster tail. Had we been on the ground, it might have seemed electrifying and terrible. But from our high vantage the scene was merely grotesque. The rioters all seemed aimless and cowardly, and the police, despite their equipment and training, cowered miserably behind their shields. To their credit, none of the cops showed any of that crowd-stomping gusto one expects from military-grade riot police, in the model of the French CRS.

Though murderous with immigrants, the CRS can be perfectly civil if you are all three of the following: white, decently dressed, and doing something the French can readily appreciate. Before we were married, my wife and I once drove out to Versailles with a picnic and found a secluded spot in the trees beside an old canal. We had heard there would be a political event of some importance at the château, and so were not surprised to see a band of six or eight CRS men approaching through the woods, combing the grounds for security hazards. They walked past us, across the narrow canal, and all of them cast a friendly and approving glance at the arrangement: *jeune couple blanc, déjeuner sur l'herbe.* One of them, the largest and most savage in appearance, gave a courtly nod. *"Bon appétit,"* he said to us, and on they strode into the trees.

The riot in Berkeley went back and forth indecisively for some time, and soon we returned to our chess game, now and again wandering out to the fire escape to check on its progress. Eventually, the police fired off some tear gas, which made an impression, and there were several arrests. Nothing came of it. A few charges, a few stitches, a brief spasm of public outcry over "police brutality," and the house in question was torn down. My friend won the chess game, but then he often did. The women never showed.

Le Fromage

After clearing our empty plates, not a speck of the lobster sauce remaining, the captain asks if we would like cheese or dessert. Why, both, we answer together, surprised that there might be an alternative. I'm with Brillat-Savarin, who wrote that "a dinner that ends without cheese is like a beautiful woman with one eye."

As has been observed, my wife will walk through coals — or at least across the city, her cheese journal in her purse — for a round of good Camembert or a Livarot, and I would sooner be stricken instantly with gout than forgo the craftsmanship of Gilles Bajolle. On our last extended stay in France, Erin single-handedly tracked down every notable cheese shop in Paris over many months, returning with five or six of the best cheeses in stock and taking copious notes on the results. With no disrespect to its eminent founder, we were more than disappointed by Androuët, whose now dismal shop on the rue d'Amsterdam, tended by an ill-informed clerk, its window disgraced by plastic simulacra of Bries and Camemberts, provided us with a king's ransom of nearly inedible cheese. At this writing, pulling my wife's cheese journal from the cookbook shelf, I am reminded that Androuët's Tomme d'Abondance was "rubbery and flavorless," the Sancerre "chalky," and the Explorateur "completely lacking in flavor or character." The Camembert, though from Normandy, was "terrible." An off day for a celebrated *fromagerie*, perhaps, but we never returned. Pierre Androuët, son of founder Henri Androuët and author of *The Complete Encyclopedia of French Cheeses*, sold the shop to the conglomerate that owns Air France some time ago; they may have hired baggage handlers to select the cheeses.

Barthélemy, its walk-in closet of a shop on the rue de Grenelle packed to the rafters with some 240 different cheeses, received top marks, especially for its Saint-Nectaire and its famed Roquefort de la Maison Coulet—the best Roquefort we've had before or since. Our favorite *fromagerie* in Paris was that of Christian Cantin on the rue de Lourmel (his daughter Marie-Anne Cantin owns an equally fine shop on the rue du Champ-de-Mars). Among others, Cantin's Reblochon, Pont-l'Évêque, Livarot, Beaufort, and Fourme d'Ambert were consistently among the finest of their kinds. I will never forget the Camembert we brought home from Mr. Cantin on that first visit, and expect never to have a better cheese in all my life. We ate the whole round at once, wedge after wedge with some wine and a little baguette, silent but for our rapturous groans. To this day, the mere utterance of the name Cantin will set my mouth to watering.

Since de Gaulle asked Churchill how one could possibly govern a country that produces 324 different cheeses, France has only become more unruly. Although a 1989 estimate of 750 varieties may be overly exuberant, most experts seem to agree that there are now in the neighborhood of five hundred French cheeses, a number that fluctuates as new artisanal cheeses appear and others vanish. All this from a count, in 1777, of some thirty known varieties. Of the existing five hundred, a mere thirty-four are name-controlled at this writing. Applied to dairy, wine, *eaux-de-vie,* and other farm goods, AOC status (Appellation d'Origine Contrôlée) guarantees that a given product is produced in a specific area by specific means. For cheeses, that may include regulations regarding the quality of milk, the time of curing, and the shape, size, and color of the finished cheese.

How long cheese goes back is unclear. In the neighborhood of 10,000 B.C., when goats and sheep were first domesticated, their herdsmen must have discovered the natural process by which souring milk will separate into curds and whey. By accident or inspiration, someone must have drained off the whey and allowed the curds to dry, fashioning the first known cheese. It is likely that the curdling characteristics of gastric secretions were discovered by chance, when an ancient herder stored fresh milk in a bag made from the stomach of a kid or lamb. Rennin is the responsible enzyme in rennet; this substance is so effective that one part of pure rennin will coagulate five million parts of milk. Cave paintings in the Libyan Sahara dating from 5000 B.C. show what appears to be concerted cheese-making. Actual cheese residue—hard evidence—has been discovered in an Egyptian pot dating from 2300 B.C. Reconstituted with a little warm water, I'm sure this bit of history would be far more savory than the hardened, splitting heels of generic cheddar, abandoned unwrapped in a refrigerator drawer, together with Velveeta and American and the so-called Swiss, as rubbery as it was insipid, that passed as cheese on the collective tables of our suburban New York town, circa 1975. Beside such a cheese board, a nondescript delicatessen provolone struck the palate as exotic.

Mesopotamian scribes would have us believe that they enjoyed some twenty different cheeses. Homer, ever keen with ethnographic detail, wrote of cheese in the *Odyssey:* the Cyclops Polyphemus included cheese-making among his talents. Having already stolen a few of his cheeses for their supper, Odysseus and his companions watch the giant curdle sheep and goat milk and pour the curd into wicker baskets. It is from the Greek word for such a basket, *formos,* that we inherit the French *fromage* and the Italian *formaggio* (and doubtless the French *former,* to give shape, and *forme,* which lost an "e" while crossing the English Channel in 1066). Cheese makes more than one appearance in Homer's epic; in the following chapter, the goddess Circe mixes her potion of forgetfulness into a pottage of cheese, barley-meal, honey, and wine, and serves it to the men of Odysseus' reconnaissance party before polymorphing them into grunting pigs. In 42 B.C., Virgil wrote of fresh cheese served with fruit and chestnuts. The use of rennet as a curdling agent was certainly established before the rise of Rome, whose citizens often breakfasted on goat cheese with bread. The legionnaires received cheese as part of their daily ration, and Julius Caesar reportedly ate a blue cheese at the village of Saint-Affrique, near Roquefort. In 65 A.D., Columella wrote that milk "should be curdled with rennet obtained from a lamb or kid, though it can be done with the flower of the wild thistle or the seeds of the safflower, and equally well with the liquid which flows from a fig-tree if you make an incision in the bark while it is still green."

To make cheese, a quantity of milk is warmed to a set temperature, starter bacteria and rennet are added, and the milk curdles. The specific bacteria used as a starter will determine much of the cheese's final flavor and consistency. To help separate the firmer curds from the liquid whey, the curds are often cooked, salted, cut, and drained. They are milled and pressed to remove more whey, then shaped into their characteristic forms: drums or wheels or squares or, more rarely, unusual shapes like hearts, bells, cones, or pyramids. In the final stages of production, molds or bacteria are added, and with the exception of fresh varieties like feta, ricotta, and fromage blanc, the cheese ages in a controlled environment over a period of weeks or months.

As anyone with taste buds will tell you, there is no comparison in flavor between raw-milk cheeses and their pasteurized cousins. Pasteurization kills much of the cheese's inherent flavor, a fact that cheese makers in the United States have accepted and applied with great success. In places like Marin and Sonoma Counties,

California, artisanal raw-milk cheeses are making an enormous comeback.

I have always been wary of cute cheeses, suspecting that what they boast in geometric novelty they must lack in character. The modest, lovely round of a Livarot or Saint-Nectaire (a form shared by countless other varieties) is my favorite shape in a cheese, being the most humble and pastoral to the eye, and the easiest to cut and eat. I have always felt a similar affection for the squares of Pont-l'Évêque, their diagonal halves evoking the neatly cut sandwiches of childhood. And it is true that the enormous, intact drums of Cantal, say, or wheels of Gruyère, standing like cyclopean stones in the windows of a cheese shop, hold an awesome fascination for the passerby. Massive, dense, pure in shape, rich in subdued color, their smooth skins are beautified by printed stamps of authenticity as if by henna paintings. It is somehow painful to see such a wheel go under the double-handled knife for the first time, to see its round perfection compromised, its Alpine heart exposed to the Parisian air. I have always wanted to buy an entire eighty-five-pound wheel of the finest Gruyère—though I shudder to imagine its four-figure cost—and carry it home across my shoulders like a spoil of war. I suspect that I would never presume to cut it. It would desiccate and grow dusty beneath my admiration, and that wouldn't do, for cheeses long to be eaten.

In France, cheeses are customarily served first to the host, who inspects them and cuts the first wedge from any whole cheeses in the assembly. This spares the well-mannered guest the discomfiture of assaulting an intact Camembert.

Why Americans so often serve bread and cheese as an hors d'oeuvre before dinner is another mystery: the last thing you should start a meal with is a rich, fatty food that will spoil your appetite.

At 11:00, minutes after setting new plates, the captain and a server in a white jacket appear bearing two large cheese trays between them. There are more than a dozen varieties on each tray, of cow and goat cheeses respectively, and the captain invites us to choose four apiece. Erin is dismayed to find no Camembert in the assembly. The captain explains that the restaurant does not offer Camembert because the name itself is not origin-controlled. Faux Camemberts are made in Ohio and Texas, among other places, and only 6 percent of the Camemberts sold in France are AOC. These are stamped with tags that read "VCN" (Véritable Camembert de Normandie). In any case, Erin decides on a Saint-Nectaire, a Chèvre Briquette, a Livarot, and a Cantal. Ever since she stumbled upon the Saint-Nectaire of all Saint-Nectaires at a farmers' market in the Fifteenth Arrondissement six years ago, she has been on a quest to find its rival. I choose a Pont-l'Évêque—one of my perennial favorites—a Fourme d'Ambert, a Crottin de Chavignol and a Pierre Robert. The captain cuts each cheese with a different silver knife, and serves them with a basket of dinner rolls and *pain de mie*.

Dating from the thirteenth century, Pont-l'Évêque

may well be the oldest and noblest of the so-called monastery cheeses, those varieties, including Münster and Havarti, first produced in early European monasteries and convents. Although the most popular varieties have inspired tasteless factory imitations, monastery cheeses are still made by religious orders, most of them in France, Belgium, Switzerland, and Germany. Monastery cheeses, though all distinct in character, are all semisoft, cow's-milk, washed-rind cheeses made from uncooked curds. The French rank Pont-l'Évêque the fourth of their great cheeses, behind Brie, Camembert, and Roquefort. Shaped into squares an inch and a half thick, less than four and a half inches on a side, it has a distinctively textured rind that turns orange as it ripens. The *pâte,* or paste, of a fully mature Pont-l'Évêque glistens with fat when cut. Its flavor is rich, complex, and tangy, yet not overpowering. It has a delicious and mild earthy scent, and might be the perfect Norman cheese for those who like full-flavored cheeses but are put off by the particular potency of a ripe Camembert, a cheese lauded for its odor by French Surrealist poet Léon-Paul Fargue as *les pieds de Dieu*—the feet of God. (Camembert is hardly the most forward of cheeses; some varieties, like the creamy A Filetta of Corsica, can burn the eyes.) Although Ireland claims to make a version, the true Pont-l'Évêque is in little danger of imitation: the bacteria that give the cheese its flavor refuse transplantation from the cellar walls in Normandy where it is produced.

The Auvergne gives us Saint-Nectaire, another monastery cheese, with a reddish, inedible rind. A favorite of Louis XIV, it was described by one writer as having a taste combining elements of walnut, copper, and spices. Its scent is earthy and grassy, and some claim to smell the rye straw on which the cheese is aged. It is formed into disks more than eight inches in diameter and two inches thick.

The Crottin de Chavignol is a semihard goat cheese made in the hamlet of Chavignol, in Berry. The word *crottin* means horse or mule droppings, to the amusement of French schoolchildren. The name was adopted for the small round barrel-like form of the cheese, a shape that is in my view only vaguely reminiscent of its name.

Cantal, often and erroneously called the French cheddar, hails from the department of the same name in the Auvergne. When formed, the cheeses are shaped like beer kegs, and the largest can weigh as much as a hundred pounds. It is said to have the scent of the high meadows of the Auvergne. Cantal, or a cheese like it, has been with us since the Romans. Pliny the Elder describes a similar cheese made near Lozère.

At Taillevent, the cheeses are superb to the last, although the Saint-Nectaire, while excellent, fails to top the cheese from the unknown farmer that was sold in the Fifteenth. By the time the empty plates have been cleared away, we are in a state of caloric shock. I have never actually eaten a horse, but this must be how it feels to do so. Despite the fact that I'm not sure if I can rise from the table when the time comes, it is in the main a pleasurable sensation. I feel drugged, less from the wine than from the amount of energy required by digestion. After reproduction, digestion requires more physical energy than any other natural human act. Thanks to the countless buds, or villi, texturing the folds of the intestinal wall, an average human being has an intestinal surface area rivaling that of a football field. I have overeaten to the point of discomfort on many occasions, but I have never eaten so well and so steadily for so long at one sitting. I am less stuffed than meticulously packed. It is 11:15; we have been here for two and three-quarters hours, eating steadily. Or I have. Normally a trencherman of note, capable on a given night of eating me under the table, my wife has found her appetite mysteriously subdued all evening. Nerves, perhaps, or the richness of the fare, or too many gougères in the first inning. Determined to see nothing sent back, I have eaten more than a third of her dinner, course after course, and all of mine. Nonetheless, we believe we have room for dessert. I will find room, by God. I will grow another stomach. I take a sip of Volvic as a lubricant, work the muscles of my stomach invisibly once or twice, kneading and compressing its contents, and try to produce a silent belch. After several attempts I summon forth a little inaudible bleed of air and, with another twitch or two of the diaphragm, something shifts, providing the illusion if not the fact of more capacity.

There is something more than a little vulgar about all this, of course, something shameful and excessive and marvelous about eating so much food of such quality, like talking an exceptionally refined young woman you've just met into spending all day and night for three straight days in her apartment—showering now and then *à deux,* eating wordlessly out of containers—until the apartment looks as if it had been sacked and occupied by a platoon of Italian mercenaries. After a few days, the world beyond her drawn shades—now pale, now black—grinds to a seemingly irrevocable halt. Like that, instead of taking her to a few proper meals first, *Becket* at the Comédie-Française, a late night of trespassing at Père Lachaise, something. If there is a regrettable aspect to our meal's excess at Taillevent, in my present state of mind I've lost sight of it, for the appetites, let run, are equipped with their own moral anesthetic, knowing only a want and its momentary satisfaction.

In fact, that's not entirely true. Though I have more or less ignored the sense that there may be something wrong with eating so much, and at such expense, it does tickle the back of my brain like a spider. It's certainly not a crime to eat well, or even to support what in effect is an art form, the modesty of some cooks notwith-standing. If one should be so fortunate, I would like to think a decent life could bear the weight of more than one such meal. Yet, when I try to imagine, among my circle of acquaintances, the half-dozen or so people I most admire eating at Taillevent, the people who *appear* to be living (or have lived) their lives most honorably, I cannot. These are mostly Americans, but not all of them. One is a Dutch expatriate in Connecticut.

Distinct in manner and interests, they all seem to share a certain natural restraint, and live, whatever their financial circumstances, simply. They are none of them in the slightest bit showy, and extravagant only in feeling. And while they instinctively avoid excess, they seem to enjoy life to a degree I find astonishing. One is a novelist and gardener, another a painter, a third an Orthodox Christian relief worker. Each of them would appreciate a good meal profoundly, as they seem to have a particular reverence for minor phenomena. But for the life of me I cannot imagine any one of them ever thinking to eat at a three-star restaurant. It simply wouldn't occur to them, I suspect, and if it did, or was proposed, they'd politely let the suggestion pass. Yet here I sit, engorged and exultant.

One thing that nags me, even as the evening unfolds, is how unusual this meal is, how rare a thing. It occupies, in the range of human dietary experience, the very farthest of two ends of a spectrum. Though I have been extremely hungry, I have only been hungry as a lark, or as a test of will. There's certainly no harm in fasting now and again, by purpose or by chance, or in curtailing or eliminating this or that, for the inevitably righteous "health and personal reasons." But such abstemiousness in no way resembles actual hardship. I've always had a hot meal, as it were, in the pack. I have been hungry in the way that professional mountaineers have been cold and exhausted, trapped on a ridge by a storm. Voluntarily, more or less for the fun of it, and not at all in the way that Tibetan refugees, fleeing over those same mountains with their children on their backs, can become cold and exhausted, trapped on a ridge. The cold and fatigue are the same, the animal fear of dying may be the same, but the experience is worlds apart.

I consciously deny the natural suspicion, generally called by philosophers the Conservation of Joy, that there is only so much love and contentment and anguish in the world, and that by suffering we relieve others of suffering, that in happiness we deprive others of happiness. It's a fair enough mistake. We are forced to count beans endlessly in the physical world: there are only so many s'mores to go around, and we can't all sit in Mom's lap at the same time. But even though I'm as prey to greed and envy as the next man, in the realm of emotion and spirit I categorically do not believe this to be true. Metaphysically, there is an endless supply of cod-liver oil out there, an endless supply of whipped cream. Food *is* beans, however, and what I eat, another may not. Nutritionally speaking, life does begin to feel like a zero-sum game. If this is so, I wonder, who now serves as my counterweight? What village, what town has been set out to starve—it's really just a flicker I dismiss—that I may eat more than my fill? Arguably, a traditional Frenchman would never have this internal conversation. He would find no need to justify an extravagant meal. He would simply enjoy it, unfettered by a Puritan pang.

Le Dessert

The captain approaches, the agent of our undoing, and hands us our menus. The desserts, *les Entremets de Douceur*, are on the back page.

Farandole de Desserts
Sablé aux Épices et aux Fraises des Bois
Mille-Feuille aux Fruits rouges et aux deux
  Vinaigres
Terrine de Fruits au Miel safrané
Sorbets aux trois Parfums
Fantaisie aux Pêches et à la Verveine
Sorbet à la Pomme verte et au Basilic
Cassolette de Fruits à la Mélisse
Griottes de Fougerolles en Chaud-Froid
Dacquoise en Surprise
Moelleux au Chocolat et au Thym
Fondant lacté au Citron confit
Crème brûlée à la Bergamote
Marquise au Chocolat et à la Pistache
Soufflé chaud aux Abricots
Crêpes soufflées au Citron vert

A long list. Still gluttonous and lamenting the impossibility of choice, we finally agree on a half-order of the *fantaisie aux pêches*, a half-order of the *mille-feuille* to try Bajolle's puff pastry, and a whole *moelleux au choco-*

lat for us to share. The captain nods and retreats. In a flash, a *chef de rang* neatens the table and clears it of unnecessary silver, glasses, and the empty wine bottle. The decks have been cleared for the final action. We sit torpid as lizards in a beating sun, gazing absently at the other diners, watching the servers appear not to watch the tables, wondering at the ghastly abstract spatter of a painting on the opposing wall. The work is ugly in the plainest terms, the way a stretch of cobbled gutter where a large dog has been sick is ugly. Yet there it hangs, in a dining room that everywhere else cries out with period restraint. Vrinat must have approved it— he may even have bought it—Vrinat, within whose otherwise impeccable dream we are dining, whose taste by this point in the meal is beyond reproach.

In the pastry kitchen upstairs, Jérôme Pendaries works alone, finishing the last orders. Pendaries is Bajolle's full-time *commis pâtisserie*, and he is sufficiently skilled to be left in charge after the departure of Bajolle's *sous-chef*, Jean-David Debras. Pendaries has been at Taillevent for four months.

Bajolle is the first to arrive in the early morning, and spends the first part of the day preparing ingredients for the lunch desserts. He works during the lunch service, plating desserts and overseeing the presentations of his staff. In the afternoon, he prepares for dinner. The critical work finished, he leaves the restaurant in the early evening, surrendering the dinner desserts' presentation to the hands of his staff. I once confessed surprise to Bajolle at such an arrangement. No matter how skilled his inferiors, should he not be present to cast an eye across each dessert as it departs? He shook his head. "I have done everything required by the time I leave the kitchen," he said. "The elements are all prepared. All that remains is to construct the desserts according to my directions. There are only one or two desserts where a careful dosage is required at the time of presentation— the vinegars on the *mille-feuille*, for example—and my cooks are capable of that. If they weren't, I would never leave them."

The two half-desserts appear ten minutes later, at 11:35, with small silver trays of chocolates and petits-fours. True to form, neither dessert appears to have been halved. The sommelier materializes and pours us each a brimming glass of honey-colored muscat from a bottle labeled with the Taillevent mark—another offering from the house. The pause has worked wonders. Together, we plunge into the pale verbena ice cream, peaked atop the deep-red peaches of the *fantaisie*.

And there it is, the raison d'être of this entire operation, the reason for our presence here, for the outlandish expense. In what has indeed proved the best single meal of our lives, this ice cream is the crowning taste. We grope mentally for precedents and find none. It is better than Cantin's Camembert, better even than Legendre's lobster and chestnuts, and I am awestruck.

Why it is so good I do not know. But it manages to be wondrously sweet and lemony without being too much of either, and fat and creamy as molecularly possible without seeming at all heavy. It is flawlessly balanced, and thus perfect, at least on this occasion, and the palate knows that it has met perfection as surely as we know when our hair has caught fire after leaning directly over a gas burner to light a cigarette. This didn't happen to me, I'm happy to report, but to a friend who sensibly moved to Switzerland and took up massage therapy.

In the culinary realm, this ice cream feels a bit like the first time you respond consciously to Mozart, when you realize that all other creative efforts, of all time and in any field, are somehow naught in comparison with these simple notes, strung together and played on instruments built by man. It is an unearthly sound, the lamentation of angels, yet there it is, alive in the air. I'm not suggesting that this ice cream, though flawless, has either the artistic merit or the effect of Mozart's best work, for the palate is not as closely connected to our higher faculties, generally speaking, as our hearing, sight, or smell. I cannot imagine any food affecting me to the degree that the Parthenon has, or Yeats, or the scent of my first girlfriend's shampoo, circa July of 1978, deep in the folds of a blue cotton sweater.

Perhaps I give our sense of taste a shorter shrift because it is purely sensual. The soul rises to a meal, when it rises, not through its flavors, however sublime, but through its companionship and setting. Wine helps. I have had better meals, in this sense, with my dog, splitting a sandwich on a roadside in Nevada, than with human relatives with whom I feel less at ease. Best, of course, is to gather with people dear to me and to eat and drink well together—on some level, it hardly matters what's on the table. One of my favorite meals in memory occurred the first time I took my daughter, not quite two at the time, out to dinner. We went to the Home Port back door in Menemsha on a warm September evening and for the price of a Boston whaler took a brown bag of lobster with melted butter, a pint of quahog chowder, fries, coleslaw, and a slice of Key lime pie, all perfectly tasty but unremarkable except for the chowder, which is invariably superb. We drove around to the beach and sat in the sand against the stones of the jetty to eat and watch the sunset. My daughter loved everything, even the coleslaw, despite the sand and wind, and so did I. Were I on my deathbed allowed to relive one of my life's meals in its entirety, exactly as it occurred, that would almost definitely be the meal. But we are all different, certainly, and I suspect there are some whose palates are so finely attuned that they can taste the transcendent through bread alone.

My wife is feeling precisely the same way, I see, about the ice cream. She looks shaken, incredulous. "This is the best thing I've ever tasted," she says. How an ice cream or a sweet of any kind could possibly surpass a savory masterpiece like the lobster and chestnuts, or the *sauce poulette*—until thirty seconds ago the best things *I* had ever tasted—is well beyond me, particularly for my palate. I do have a reasonably aggressive sweet tooth, and will often bake up a double batch of honey madeleines to be eaten hot, and can absentmindedly plow through half a bag of Oreos with milk at a sitting. I comfort myself with the fact that two dozen

Oreos have no more fat than eight tablespoons of traditional mayonnaise, and little more than six tablespoons
of straight olive oil. They also taste better. Nonetheless,
if you catch me at an odd, hungry moment, I'll always
take a savory dish over a sweet—a really good lobster
roll, perhaps, with a boat of shoestring fries. In the
pick-one-thing-to-eat-on-a-desert-island scenario, my
top ten edible candidates would all be savory, and most
of them would be running with fat of some kind or
another. Good brownies—and I would have thrown
the switch on Albert Schweitzer for one of my Kansas-
born maternal grandmother's warm brownies—would
probably come in around number fourteen. On the subject of my grandmother, a friend of James Beard's who
cooked and entertained without cease, her *Soupe du Roi*
(King's Soup) was unimpeachable. He must have been a
heavy king. Ostensibly a pea soup, it is both 100 percent
cream and 100 percent butter, and it is extraordinary.
How she managed to squeeze a little salt, sugar, egg
yolk, and puréed peas into an already fractionally impossible recipe is beyond me, but who am I to quibble with
success?

"All recipes have stories behind them," Bajolle once
told me. "And if they do not, you must build a story
around an idea." As an adolescent in rural France, he
said, he had fallen in love with a young woman, somewhat older than he, of many talents. I immediately
imagined the seductress in the bowler hat in the film of
The Unbearable Lightness of Being. This woman, whom

he did not name, wore a subtle verbena perfume, manufactured by Descamps. The perfume no longer exists, although he found a different brand with the same scent more recently. Some seven or eight years ago, Bajolle decided to do something with the herb in memory of this woman, who now lives, he said, "on the other side of the globe." If Bajolle were a native Parisian, this might mean Strasbourg or Lyon, but since he hails from the French countryside, I expect she may have moved to Germany. She had perpetually cold skin, he said, *la peau du serpent,* and since scents respond differently to skins of different temperatures, an ice cream seemed most appropriate. The ice cream must taste, to some degree, the way she smelled. Fortunate would be the traveler to share a nonsmoking compartment with her on the Orient Express to Istanbul.

Bajolle had also tasted a dessert of peaches flavored with green tea at another restaurant, and decided to replace the green tea with verbena. The herb, being seasonal, arrives in boxes of two or three hundred bunches. He infuses it in milk and deep-freezes the milk in pouches to use throughout the year.

"The verbena comes from Tours," he said. "The big problem is being in Paris. It's not like being in the provinces. I once spent a week *chez* Trois Gros. In the morning, you can go directly to the farmer, or to the small markets. Last week, in Cannes, I went with the chef to the market; just across the street were all the merchants. You could try a strawberry—'Hmm. His strawberries aren't as good today'—*hop*, you go to the next stall. Here in Paris, we get on the phone. 'Is the fruit good?' we ask. 'Oh sure. No problem,' they say. You see? At its roots, cuisine is from the country.

"Another problem," said Bajolle, "is that the menus at Taillevent last for four or five months, and it's difficult to have peaches over five months. Meat is fine. You can put rabbit and veal and beef on the menu all year. It's always available. But grapes, peaches, apricots—they all have a specific season. And if we have a dessert with peaches, like the *fantaisie*, the peaches must always be of the same quality. Which means they must be canned. So I went to someone in the southwest of France and explained what I wanted, and he chose a peach that keeps very well in a can. A special variety, very old, called *pêche de Carman*. He cans them for us, and, thanks to the qualities of this peach, we can make the dessert year-round.

"To give more flavor to the peaches, we cook their juice with cassis. When the juice has cooled, we mix it with peach pulp, and add a little maraschino liqueur to bring out the flavor. Then we add mint, very finely chopped, for freshness, and when we pour the sauce over the peaches they take on a violet color. We prepare the peaches every day. The ice cream itself is an infusion, like a verbena *crème anglaise*, to which we add small flecks of lime zest."

To compose the dessert, the ice cream is funneled through a serrated pastry nozzle into a small, cup-shaped cookie, called a tulip, made of flour, sugar, egg whites, butter, and shaved pistachio. Stewed peaches in their juice surround the tulip.

I found the tulip cookies to be one of the more daunting tasks I fell foul of as an apprentice in Bajolle's kitchen. The batter is perilously thin and poured out on a cookie sheet like miniature crêpes, each perhaps three and a half inches in diameter. The pistachio shavings are sprinkled atop them, and the cookies bake for a few minutes, until their edges just begin to turn golden. Time is now of the essence. Armed with a mold in the form of a small glass bowl, you must open the oven door and pluck each cookie, hot as molten brass and limp as a damp doily, from the sheet, then press it swiftly into the bowl to form a suggestively floral vessel before it cools. If you do not press it into the bowl quickly and firmly enough—and you do not—the tulip will be too shallow, or it will break through at the bottom under your thumb as you race against the cookie's plummeting plasticity. If this were not enough, I began by pressing the cookie too firmly along the bowl's upper edges, crushing flat what became in Bajolle's hands a serpentine, elegantly floral perimeter. My primary problem, never surmounted, was that the thin golden disks were too hot to handle at the outset, and I seared my unaccustomed fingertips on the cookie sheet each time I plunged in for another. For his part, Bajolle seemed to whisk them up and out of the oven without ever coming into contact with the cookie sheet, and with a fluid motion had whipped each into a perfect and uniform tulip before you could say, "Ow, son of a bitch." This is a man who could pull eggs from boiling water with his hands, I reflected, and there's nothing quite like doing something four or five thousand times to work out the kinks.

"The story of the *mille-feuille* is much simpler," Bajolle tells me, "because it is such a classic. There is the problem we discussed of the menu, which may last three, four, or five months. So we must find products available throughout this period. Also, we must send out the desserts very quickly. So we do the desserts at Taillevent because they're practical and fast. We could do many other desserts, but we don't have the time or resources to prepare them. Like the *tarte à café*, which is sometimes on the menu. If we make twenty and sell only one, the rest will not keep. They'll be thrown out, or go to the staff, and the restaurant will lose money. So the menu is made relative to the availability of the product, and to the time the dish requires to prepare. We cannot sustain a loss.

"In the *mille-feuille*, the butter is very important. We have someone who delivers our butter. We tasted many varieties. Then we worked the *mille-feuille* to improve it, because you can have good butter and good flour but the way you cook the dough is no less important. The *feuilletage* itself takes three days. On the first day, you make the dough; the following day, you turn it over; and the third day, you roll it and lay it out on a tray. Everything must be perfect—every step, every link in the chain. This is true for all these desserts. For the verbena ice cream, even if the verbena is excellent, it won't work if you overcook the cream. You can give someone recipes, but if they don't have the same products, and the same techniques, and the same palate, the results will be different. That's what's so interesting. Otherwise, it would be too easy. It would become merely industrial."

The *mille-feuille* is a favorite at Taillevent. During one lunch service, an order for five of them comes into the pastry kitchen. Debras, Pendaries, and Yoann Chevet, a trainee who normally works in the main kitchen, create an assembly line. Debras sets out the plates and squeezes a small dose of *crème à la rose* into the middle of each plate to serve as an anchor. He spoons sliced strawberries out of a pot and makes a ring of them around the inside edge of the plate. The strawberries have been marinating in a blend of orange juice, mint, cinnamon, vanilla, and sugar, as well as the extracts of eleven other plants and flowers, including hibiscus, mango, eucalyptus, and bitter orange.

Beside Debras, Pendaries draws a generous bead of rose cream atop the perimeter of a square of baked puff pastry, three inches on a side. Quickly, in twos, he sets raspberries side by side into the square of cream. He fills the middle of the square with raspberries one layer deep. Then he squeezes a dollop of cream in the middle of the berries, to adhere to the layer above. When he has finished, Debras takes the square and places it gently in the middle of the plate, square atop the anchor of cream. Debras, while he works, stands with his back straight, head bowed. Pendaries bows low over the counter from the waist, his back curved, his eyes not a foot above his work. Chevet, meanwhile, prepares the second layer, prepared like the first but with small, wild strawberries instead of raspberries. This layer, too, receives a dollop of cream in its center. The second layer is set atop the first. The third and final square of puff pastry is dusted with confectioner's sugar on a separate plate and set on top. The result is a perfect triple-decker sandwich. Just before he sets them on a tray to put in the dumbwaiter, Debras sprinkles a little balsamic vinegar and raspberry vinegar onto the cut fruit.

"The *mille-feuille* is very traditional," says Bajolle, "but we have made a few changes. The *crème à la rose* is new. Earlier this year, we added rose syrup and gelatin to vanilla pastry cream. Before that we tried many things, but it was very difficult to find the right flavor. And then we use the two vinegars, in small amounts, to draw out the flavor of the fruit.

"You see how quickly we need to prepare them. That is a problem. I believe it's necessary to find a way to make things more calmly, to be sure of the proper dosage. That is the biggest problem with flavorings that must be added at the last instant. You need to be able to find the right proportion. With a dessert like *pêches à la verveine*, there is no danger. All is prepared in advance, and if you add a little more or less of one element— more peach, or more ice cream—it will not change the taste of the dessert. But with the *mille-feuille*, if someone is rushing and adds too much vinegar, it will certainly affect the flavor.

"With many desserts," he says, "including the *mille-feuille*, one must take care to preserve the individual flavors of the ingredients. With raspberries, for example, you must add the vanilla sugar and the anise at the very last instant, so the client will taste each flavor. Another example is the *charlotte aux fraises*. Classically, there is cookie around the cake, and inside there is strawberry mousse, but you must not make it that way. You must put the cookie on the top and on the bottom, and between them put a good vanilla cream and sliced whole strawberries. You must layer it: cream, strawberries, cream, strawberries. This way you will taste all the flavors in a single bite. If you make a mousse, and blend the strawberries with sugar and cream, when you taste it the strawberry will have lost its potency. There are many products that you cannot crush and mix with other things, because the taste will change completely. When you make a mousse of apricot, strawberry, or raspberry, you're going to add cream, sugar, and egg whites, and the flavor of the fruit will naturally diminish. Like the apricot soufflé. You add a little sugar and egg whites; but the egg whites have no flavor, so it borrows flavor from the apricot. Therefore, you must add *alcool de noyaux* to enhance the flavor of the apricot. If there's no alcohol, you will not taste the apricot."

During our meal, the *fantaisie* is an impossible act to

follow. The *mille-feuille*, while exquisite, cannot compare. The pastry itself is extraordinary, the *crème à la rose* superb, but the strawberries themselves, at least today, are a bit too tart. In nearly any other restaurant, this *mille-feuille* would represent an enduring high point in our culinary experience. But we have been successively spoiled by Legendre and Bajolle, one course after another, and even the faintest deviation from perfect balance is startling.

Bajolle was born in February of 1959 in the department of Le Gers, in the southwestern region of Gascogne. The eldest of three, he describes his childhood as friendless and "completely isolated." I am surprised at this admission, because in his kitchen he could hardly be more gregarious. "When other young people went to bars," he said, "I stayed home in the garage and worked on engines, bicycles, electrical devices. I loved building things, figuring out how things worked. I didn't read much until later. I was happier working with my hands.

"As a child, I always wanted to understand why things were done a certain way. Why you must build a roof like this and not like that. Why a staircase curves a certain way. Why electricity works. Why such-and-such a taste? Why do we need to add salt or sugar? I really wanted to understand what people had tried to do in the past. That's why I continue to visit other kitchens, to try new things, to learn more.

"Through history, we have always sought to make something beautiful, something rational, something that serves a purpose. When they built churches in the Middle Ages, and erected huge columns, they were visually heavy. So they discovered a form that was just as functional but attractive to the eye. Of course the column must support a load. But they found a way to decorate the column, so that it looked not so much massive as it did beautiful. It's extraordinary. I love the gargoyles on the waterspouts, and the flying buttresses. The buttresses are structurally required, very strong, but beautiful and light to the eye. Now we do everything quickly. We put up buildings clac, clac, clac, so of course it's very hard to make them attractive. The buildings on the outskirts of Paris, for example. They're like rabbit cages—it's terrible. That kind of architecture alone can make the inhabitants unwell."

Bajolle dabbled in painting and wood sculpture, and studied briefly with a local metalworker. He suspects that he inherited his mother's potent sense of smell. A gardener and a superb cook, she often crushed herbs between her fingers and asked him to identify them by their scents. "As a child I was more habituated to the smells of women than of men," he said. "I love the smell of wood, of plants. I love the smell of cement. I prefer things in balance; if it's too strong or too faint, I don't like it. The color and smell of blood are too violent. That's why I don't work in the *cuisine*. The smells— *ris de veau*, for example—are too heavy, too strong." When an American apprentice, Sarah Watts, arrived for work that morning, Bajolle knew she had switched perfumes the moment she came through the door.

Watts is a twenty-two-year-old redhead from Seattle, Washington. She is near the end of a two-year program in culinary arts at a local community college, and took time off to do a long apprenticeship at Taillevent. She wrote fifty letters to French restaurants in Paris and received twenty-six responses, many of them dubious. Only two of the responses seemed professional, one from the two-star restaurant Laurent on the Avenue Gabriel, and one from Bajolle. On arriving in France this past March, she met Bajolle first, and has been at Taillevent for five months. Watts is pretty, pale, and curvaceous, and might be a model for Rubens in her apron and white pastry jacket. Unsurprisingly, she is a target for good-natured flirtation from some members of the cooking staff, although I never see or hear anything offensive—unexpected, given the overlapping reputations of Frenchmen and professional cooks. Nor is there any hazing or sexist innuendo in evidence; they all seem fond of her, and happy to have a cheerful young woman in their midst. She is also a good sport: she politely flirts back. Near the end of my time there, shortly before the restaurant closes for August vacation, she and Bajolle have a howling water fight with buckets in the pastry kitchen. Watts takes the brunt of it, and after one or two exchanges, she is sopping wet. Water runs down the freezer doors, drips from the marble counters. Wiping the water from his eyes, red-faced and grinning, Bajolle momentarily seems thirty years younger. "Never in my time at Taillevent," he says with glee, "never have I seen this." Nor has Vrinat, I imagine.

Watts's father runs a machine shop in Seattle, making molds for plastic injection. "He's very inventive," she said, as we made petits-fours on a marble counter. "And it shows in his cooking. He loves working with his hands, and I've inherited that." She began cooking at home at the age of eight, when her mother went to work. "I was never very good at school," she said. "I learned to read and do math through cookbooks." She plans to open her own bakery and pastry shop in the U.S.

On one of my first afternoons in the pastry kitchen, Debras constructs tiny chocolate *"caissettes"* to include with trays of petits-fours. Using a pastry bag with a serrated tip, he fills cups of hard dark chocolate—each about an inch in diameter—with a paler chocolate mousse. He turns the bag as he squeezes it, making a spiral. Atop the mousse in each cup he lays a tiny rectangular patch of candied orange peel, skin side up. They look perfect to me, but Bajolle, passing with a pot of pears, stops. The pears have been boiled with ginger, lemon, vanilla, and honey. The pears, he says, are not as good as he remembers them, the result of large-scale production. He sets down the pot, bends over the tray of *caissettes,* and adjusts the orange peels on half a dozen of them. The spiral of mousse, he points out, while not highly peaked, nonetheless comes to a point off center. The rectangular strip of peel, he says, is not to be laid randomly atop the mousse, but anchored on the point and extended back across the center. I look more closely; Bajolle is correct. The randomly placed peels, though centered, appear somehow messy and disconnected in comparison with the corrected examples. Debras nods and continues.

If the energy in the *cuisine* is frenetic, in the *laboratoire* it cannot afford to be. The materials are often too delicate. "In pastry," says Bajolle, pretending to perch one feather-light and invisible object upon another with impossible delicacy, as if crowning an eight-story house of cards, "one must *place* things."

On another counter, Pendaries chops large bars of chocolate into crumbs and collects them in a steel bowl while another apprentice yolks eggs. Watts is busy making petits-fours. She lays out several dozen minute pie tins in a tight rectangular crowd, mists them with a nonstick spray, and lays a thin sheet of rolled dough atop them. She gently presses the sheet of dough into each cup beneath, first with a brush, then more firmly with a small wad of dough wrapped in a square of plastic wrap. Next she takes up a pair of rolling pins and rolls them firmly across the dimpled sheet of dough. The sharp rims of the pie tins appear through the dough under her pressure. Setting aside the lattice of unused dough, she hand-neatens the dough in each tin, pressing it down more deeply with her thumbs, and arranges the prepared tins on a baking rack. When baked and cooled, they will be filled with a handful of different concoctions.

Watts is not the only female apprentice to appear in

Bajolle's kitchen. Reiko Kajiwara, twenty-three, was a professional pastry chef for three years in her native Kyoto before coming to France for a three-month *stage* at Taillevent. She hopes to remain in France when her time here expires, and find work as a pastry artist, designing ornate desserts.

When he has finished the pears, Bajolle toasts chopped almonds and hazelnuts on a cookie sheet, then pours white sugar into a huge beaten-copper pot. More than a hundred years old, the hemispherical vessel looks like a battered Grecian shield, its surface pocked and lumpy. Bajolle puts the sugar in the pot over the fire and stirs it with vigor. It soon caramelizes, turning thick and golden, and Bajolle combines it with the toasted nuts to make a *nougatine*.

Some things, he says, like the caramelized sugar, can only be done in small quantities. Others, like beaten egg whites, must be done in larger volumes to succeed. On the subject of fresh herbs, he says one must never *chop* them with the heel of the knife. This crushes and bruises the herbs, which then rapidly oxidize and darken. Nor may they be left exposed to the air. Mince them carefully, he says, with a slicing motion of the blade, and put them immediately into the sauce, oil, or juice for which they are intended.

He moves on to taste a bowl of soft chocolate flavored with bergamot, and nods with satisfaction. "One tastes the chocolate with bergamot and thinks, Mmm, that's good," he says. "But one doesn't know *why* it tastes good. I find that fascinating."

Given Bajolle's wide range of talents, one might expect him to have at least a passable command of English. Surprisingly, he speaks almost none at all. One morning, observing his creation of a certain dessert, I absently slip into English. "What is that called again?" I ask him. There is a pause. "Pardon?" he asks in French. "What is that dessert called again?" I repeat in English, unthinking. He looks at me blankly. "Oh, sorry," I say, laughing at my mistake, and repeat the question in French. Bajolle seems mildly ashamed of this handicap, and of his near illiteracy with computers. "I've tried to learn a bit more about computers, but they've never been particularly interesting to me," he explains. "You push a button and something happens, invisibly. I like seeing how things work."

On another day, Watts mixes a deep bowl of warm chocolate in which to dip candied strips of orange peel. The crystallized orange strips stand by on a tray, five sheets deep. Of the highest available quality, says Bajolle, the orange strips are prepared in Marseille. The chocolate must fall to a certain temperature before it is ready. Watts dips scraps of parchment paper into the chocolate and watches how quickly and in what pattern it cools. She touches the mixing spoon, glazed with chocolate, to the middle of her lower lip, one of the body's most temperature-sensitive locations. "When the chocolate is the temperature of blood," she says, "it will be ready." Soon she begins dipping the orange strips, and laying them out to cool on sheets of parchment paper. Everything seems to want to stick to everything else.

"Hard work," I observe.

"It's fun work," she says. "It's fun to go home and find chocolate behind your ears."

I ask Bajolle about the other hazards of working with chocolate. "Chocolate is child's play," he says, "but you need to know a few things." He offers us an impromptu lecture on chocolate chemistry. Depending on the proportion of milk, sugar, and cocoa-butter molecules, the chocolate must be heated to a temperature where the molecules liquefy—say, fifty-nine degrees centigrade. It must then be cooled until all of the points, or "forks," of the chocolate molecules have stopped moving. The molecules have not yet fallen into interlocking lines, however, so the chocolate must be reheated a few degrees until they jiggle into place, like the teeth of a zipper. At this point the chocolate is "tempered." When it cools, it will break cleanly, with a snap. Its color will be rich and glossy, without the grey streaking visible on chocolate that has lost its temper.

While Watts works on the chocolate, Bajolle prepares a new dessert, invented last week. It is an apple-and-lime sorbet with flecks of basil in it, served with a cookie and wings of finely sliced fresh apple. The cookie is flat as a ribbon, long as a cigar, and twisted into the shape of a corkscrew. Bajolle experiments briefly with the placement of the cookie on the plate, trying different angles and positions vis-à-vis the sorbet and the apple wings. He changes it, gazes at it vacantly for a moment, changes it again. He arrives at a position where the cookie appears weightless and dynamic, cutting up and across the ensemble, as if it had alighted for a moment like a butterfly and would, in another instant, flit away. "Like this," he tells Debras. He puts it in the dumbwaiter with four or five other desserts, rings the bell, and sends it down.

On another afternoon, Bajolle prepares *Fondant lacté au Citron confit*. In a large mixing bowl, he prepares a mousse of milk chocolate, lemon, and bergamot tea. He sets two dozen steel hemispherical cups, each about the diameter of a tennis ball, on a black tray. The glittering silver cups rock and jingle faintly as he slides the tray across the marble counter. He fills a clear plastic disposable pastry bag with the mousse, twists it closed under his right hand, and with swift mechanical precision fills each cup half full with the mixture. He then produces a tray of thin, spongelike, circular chocolate cookies, lightly paints them on each side with lemon juice, and presses them gently, one after another, into the mousse in each cup. This accomplished, he refills the pastry bag and tops off the cups with mousse, concealing each cookie. Picking up one filled cup in each hand, holding them from above, he neatly raps them twice on the marble counter to dispel the bubbles. The steel against the marble makes a rich percussive sound, and he raps the rest of them in the same fashion. Toc-toc . . . toc-toc . . . toc-toc . . . toc-toc . . . until all two dozen have been rapped and returned to the tray. He now brings out a tray of fine, circular, dark-chocolate wafers, the exact diameter of the cups. The wafers are laid in staggered rows, touching, on white pastry paper. The chocolate itself is nearly paper-thin, and some of the disks have cracked in one or two places. Holding them with care, Bajolle sets one disk atop each silver cup, covering the mousse. When a disk has broken, he sets each piece in its place precisely, as if putting together a puzzle. Not that it matters, particularly, because this side will be facedown upon the plate, but when he is finished the cracks in the wafers cannot be seen. The tray of finished cups goes into the freezer for a time. When they have chilled, Bajolle pops the perfect hemispheres from their steel cups and lays them facedown on a tray. The color of coffee ice cream, they are not as beautiful as the silver molds themselves, but their perfect shape is striking. One imagines the fine layer of chocolate unseen against the plate, and the chocolate cookie, tinged with lemon, hovering in the midst of the mousse like a burial chamber at the heart of a barrow. Later, the hemispheres will be coated with powdery dark chocolate. It is the precision of all this, the care, that I find most telling. It represents a kind of faith that sloppiness denies, the faith that, despite the endless tearing down and vanishing of things, we must build our sand castles with care.

I learned to take care of things as a small boy, and though I am grateful for the knowledge, it was not always an easy education. In the full seasons of the Northeast, bicycles left out overnight would rust, and wooden toys would warp and mildew, so it was more important there, perhaps, than in an arid clime. When I was around six or seven, my father brought home a beautiful German glider, with huge white wings like a dragonfly's and a slender yellow fuselage trimmed with red. I loved the plane, but I left it out one evening, in one corner of our yard, beneath a tree. When my father came home that night, just at my bedtime, he sat on the edge of the bed. Ordinarily, he would rub my shoulders and sing old spiritual songs in a low voice as I fell off to sleep. "Let My People Go," "Swing Low, Sweet Chariot," "Jacob's Ladder." On this particular night, he asked me where the airplane was. I said I didn't know, and this angered him. Try to remember, he said, and I told him I couldn't. We went back and forth for a while, until he turned on the bedside light and said I would not sleep until I remembered where I had left it. Fine by me, I said, and studied the wall. When I finally drifted off under the glare of the burning lamp, my father woke me. We went on in this way for some time, me slipping back into sleep, my father gently shaking me. I don't know how many times I dozed off and was awakened. Each time I tried my best to stay awake, and eventually I began to cry. I loathed myself for it but could not resist. In any case, I was determined not to give in. To weep with anger and fatigue was one thing, to surrender another. One of these times I will fall asleep, I decided, and he will not wake me. I will wake to an extinguished light, and morning. We went through what seemed an eternity of this—I was delirious; my father grim and silent, still in his tie; my mother occasionally peering in from the adjoining bathroom, wringing her hands ineffectually, only to retreat at my father's growled command. My eldest, teenaged sister eventually woke, discovered the scene, and became hysterical. She shrieked, she wept, she called our father unimaginable names—I had never seen her, or anyone aside from our father, so angry, so utterly beside herself, and I will always be grateful to her for the depth of her feeling on that occasion. She behaved, I suppose, the way I always wanted my mother to behave at such a time. When my father leapt up off the bed in her direction, baited finally from his position beside me, I surrendered. I jumped up and stood on the bed. Stop it, I shouted. I'll find it. I ran out in my pajamas and bare feet, into the cool grass damp with dew, and found the glider in the moonlight. Outside, it was quiet and still. I could have curled up beneath the tree in the wet grass. I brought the plane in, and my father watched, subdued, as I dried it with a paper towel, taking special care with the metal parts. He apologized, but he had won, and though I hated him for it, I had learned a valuable lesson on the subject of power, sacrifice, and the proper care of things. Now, nearly thirty years later, when we visit friends in California and I pass bicycles that live outside, their rims crusted with dried mud, and see toys scattered across the grass late at night, I am shocked by a sense of deep transgression tinged with dread. I have tried, with our young children, to teach the same lesson but in different ways. Bicycles and trucks are brought in. Books are treated with care. But different means produce different results, and our five-year-old is more casual than I. As I write, a wooden children's paddle can be seen on our stone terrace, exposed to the elements. It was there last night, I am sure.

Bajolle told me that every year in France chefs and others in the food industry go to schools and introduce young children to rare foods, to French cuisine, and to the art of tasting in a tradition known as La Semaine du Goût, or The Week of Taste. One day his daughter and a classmate came into the kitchen in long aprons for a few hours of informal apprenticeship. They made cookies with small pastry bags, cut dough into circles for petits-fours, and prepared a *crème anglaise,* among other tasks. Bajolle showed them how to cut and scrape whole vanilla beans, how to yolk eggs, how to know when the cream, cooking down gently on the fire, is nearing its desired consistency. He stirred the mixture with a flat wooden spoon, then lifted the spoon into the air above the pot. He ran a fingertip through the cream that clung to the blade of the utensil. The finger leaves a clean trail, and the cream is just thick and sticky enough, with the blade perpendicular to the floor, not to flow down and cover the gap. "Do you see?" he asked the girls. "Now you know it is ready."

One morning, Bajolle hangs a white plastic tarpaulin from the shelving and across one of his counters to create a backdrop. He sets a rectangular sheet of what might be called an ultra-refined fudge brownie on a board in the middle of the covered counter and pro-

duces a motorized airbrush like those used to paint
T-shirts or automobiles. The reservoir in his airbrush is
filled with liquid chocolate, and when he starts it up
with a grating buzz, a cone of chocolate mist spatters
finely across the rectangular pastry. He waves it back
and forth, evenly coating the pastry with the gleaming
mist. Now, *that* would be fun in the privacy of one's
own kitchen, I think, and wonder if my wife would
agree to be airbrushed from neck to toe in liquid chocolate. After coating the pastry from one angle, he turns
the board ninety degrees and repeats the process. In this
way he paints the surface of the pastry from all four
directions before setting it aside to dry. Later, the rect-
angle will be cut into squares the size of postage stamps,
to be included on the trays of petits-fours. The white
tarp looks like the wall of a café hit by Basque sepa-
ratists armed with exploding chocolate rabbits.

I accompany Bajolle on a hunt for ingredients down-
stairs, in the labyrinth of walk-in freezers and storage
rooms behind the main kitchen. He hands me a wooden
drum the size of a small wastebasket containing a cylinder of butter weighing ten kilograms. It is one of the
finest butters available in France, and when we get it
upstairs and unwrap it on the marble counter, I can't
believe how beautiful it is, this perfect monolith of
cream. At Bajolle's direction, I cut up much of the drum
into huge slabs and weigh them out.

Bajolle takes a ball of dough out of a fridge and rolls
it out flat on a marble counter dusted with flour. Made
of white flour, butter, salt, and water, the dough is the

color of pale butter. Bajolle takes one of the measured slabs of fresh butter and folds it into the dough as if enclosing the butter in an envelope. Then he beats the dough with the rolling pin, hammering the butter into the dough.

"There are countless minor details in the preparation of puff pastry," he says. He points at a faint dusting of white flour near the edge of the sheet of beaten dough, picked up from the marble. "See this?" he asks. "If I left that there, the pastry would taste heavy." He sweeps it off with a large pastry brush shaped like a dust broom. "The temperature of the water matters; the temperature of the dough when you work it matters. Everything matters." He will fold and beat the dough six times after folding in the butter, allowing it to sit in the refrigerator for at least two hours between foldings.

Bajolle prepares an average of sixteen kilograms of puff pastry a week at Taillevent. He considers puff pastry to be the most important measure of a pastry chef, and does not yet allow his staff to prepare it. In the old days, he says, the last thing an apprentice would learn would be the puff pastry. It served as a kind of exam. Now this belief is no longer widespread, and the quality of puff pastry in France and the world is deteriorating. In pastry generally, he says, decoration and appearance are gaining dominance over flavor. Even in the best restaurants, it is becoming difficult to find the finest ingredients. In 1985, he visited one of the most celebrated restaurants in Los Angeles. They bought the puff pastry and the ice cream pre-made, the chocolate mousse was prepared from a powder, and there were only three whisks in the entire kitchen. "In France we are twenty or twenty-five years behind the United States in this respect," he says, "but it is starting to happen even here."

While occupied with other tasks, Bajolle often recites long recipes to his staff, which they scribble down rapidly in their pocket-sized recipe books. He never seems to pause or to err in his recitations. Long recipes seem to come as quickly to mind as a Social Security number. I ask him how many recipes he may have in his head. Thousands?

"Perhaps," he says. "But what is more important than recipes is associations—this ingredient goes with that but not with this. That is much more important than recipes."

At fourteen, largely at his father's urging, Bajolle entered the École Hôtelière in Auch, where he spent three years studying service and cuisine. The following year, he studied pastry at the École de Tarbes. It is a decision he continues to regret. "I would have preferred to work in the *beaux arts*, or to repair châteaux and churches. The kind of work you can see tomorrow." During his year in the army, he said, he wrote poetry and drank verbena tea instead of beer. "Always a bit bizarre," he says. He now lives outside Paris, in the town of Sartrouville, with his wife of sixteen years and their two children, aged thirteen and nine.

Bajolle seems to be an excellent manager and teacher, and, though an exacting perfectionist, he works well with his staff. I never see him lose his temper, although he mutters frequently about his employer. He works harder than anyone else in his kitchen, and there is no task he considers beneath him. He washes dishes, swabs counters, sweeps under freezers, mops floors. One afternoon I find him up to his elbows in the deep sinks of a small adjoining washroom, the post for a *plongeur*.

Minutes later, as I poke into drawers and freezers, he apologizes for the mess. "Tonight, at one in the morning," he assures me, "everything will be clean." Funny, everything looks immaculate to me. The light dazzles on the marble counter and silver steel cabinets. If it weren't for all the fruit and chocolate, you'd assume you were in a surgical ward.

His tendency toward order and neatness, unsurprising in a pastry chef, approaches compulsion. Relaxed when chatting over a *panaché* (beer and lemonade) at a nearby café, in his kitchen he is never still. While reciting from memory a detailed recipe for *marquise au chocolat*, he neatens and cleans every object and surface within reach. After running out of counters and cooking implements, he takes a dry cloth and individually polishes each pen, marker pen, ruler, and paper clip in the small basket of office supplies beside the counter that serves as his desk. Lean and fit, he runs in the early mornings, before work, and plays pickup soccer on weekends. Yet I gather he remains largely reclusive in his off hours, puttering around the house, building and tinkering.

"In the beginning, I did no apprenticeship," he told

me. "And I didn't grow up in a family that owned a restaurant or a pastry shop. Had I been the son of a pastry chef, I would have learned the trade much differently. But I was not accustomed, in my family, to eating a lot of pastry. On Sundays, because family would come for lunch, we would have a traditional cake at the end of the meal. Our desserts were always very traditional, and they were never overly sweet. It was rarely something we bought at the pastry shop. It was country pastry, the kinds of things you made at home, like an apple tart. There is pastry made by professionals and home pastry, and I was much more familiar with the latter. Simple things—flour, sugar, an egg, perhaps a little butter. Not too much sugar. But good fruit, full of flavor. Now people often tell me, 'Ah, your pastry is not sweet.' And that's because my palate was not formed—or *de*formed, if you like—by classical shop pastry. If you look at the menu here at Taillevent, the pastry is not classical. There is *pâte à choux*, of course, and puff pastry. But there aren't a lot of desserts with chocolate mousse, *crème au beurre*, and so forth. I make pastry from the perspective of a very simple education. No complicated fundamentals. I'm someone who eats all the time, but not too much and not too sweet. I don't like sugar. I dislike candy. I enjoyed it as a child, but now I find it *dégoulasse* [disgusting]. It doesn't taste natural. It tastes like chemicals, synthetics.

"In the old days, there were no schools, there were only apprenticeships. Two, three, four years, living with a master, so the master's home was like a second family.

He took care of the young apprentices like his own children. They slept in his house; they had a little room. It was still like that even twenty-five or thirty years ago. Today, in the provinces, it's still a little bit like that. When someone was good, the master would call a friend with a restaurant and say, 'I'm sending you someone. He's got promise.' In this way you went along, and got married and had children. You lived in the town, and didn't move, and you stayed at the same restaurant for years. In the provinces, *chez* Trois Gros, for example, or *chez* Bocuse, there are cooks who have been there for decades. In Paris, however, you can stay in the same city and work in many different restaurants. A year here, a year at a restaurant five hundred meters away. It's much easier. And now everything moves very quickly, so you must move as well. If you stay in one restaurant, and don't have a watchful eye to see what other people are up to, if you don't try other styles, the others will pass you by. So you're obliged to work this way. Restaurant owners demand that you continue to come up with new things, because the press is watching. Now a restaurant is really a business. In the old days clients were faithful to a restaurant. They were very loyal. Now the press mentions a new trend or restaurant, and the people say, 'Okay, we'll try that.' So all this has changed. People are much more open to discovering new things. I see my grandparents, who are accustomed to eating a certain kind of country cooking. If in the country I cooked a bit of *foie gras* in a pan, my grandparents would say that wasn't possible. *Foie gras* is cooked in a certain way. They would say, 'You can't cook it that way. It's disgusting.' In the old days we did everything in a certain way. Then came nouvelle cuisine in the seventies. Kiwis with raspberries with lamb — we mixed absolutely everything. Now we're much more open. We're more curious.

"In the old days a master chef would take the time to explain things to his apprentices. Now we no longer have the time. We say, 'Here's the recipe; figure it out for yourself.' It's always faster, faster. We do everything too quickly. We're productive and numerous, but everything is built around leisure. Not leisure for pleasure, but leisure for doing nothing. *Au soleil, plus bouger.* [We lie down in the sun and we don't budge.]

"Increasingly, people don't know how to work. In the old days, a *chef de cuisine* became chef around forty or forty-five years of age. Now at twenty-one and twenty-two the young are *chefs de cuisine*. They know nothing. Then, in order to become a chef, you had to do a tour of France. You had to learn all the different styles, all the different kinds of produce. That's why I like to visit other kitchens, to continue to learn, to see new things. When you knew more or less everything there was to learn in the field, you became a chef. Now everybody's a chef."

I asked him how pastry has changed in recent years.

"Pastry is becoming less and less sweet," he said, "in part because we are respecting the products themselves much more. If you add a lot of sugar, you mask the flavors of the true ingredients. You must respect the true flavors. Even chocolate. People are eating more and more bitter chocolate, and they are enjoying more and more acidic flavors. We also use less sugar because we no longer need so much of it to preserve the dessert. Before, if we made something we would need it to keep for two or three days. And if you didn't have a fridge, or if the fridge wasn't reliable, what would you do? You used more sugar as a preservative. Early in the evolution of pastry, sugar didn't exist; they used honey or molasses. So things were very potent, very sweet. This is happening in cooking as well. In the old days they made sauces with roux, with flour and butter. Now we make *jus*. Very aromatic and very, very light. When the sauces were thicker, one could keep them several days, because they could be recooked. So, for reasons of conservation, one used a certain style of cooking.

"And yet a little bit of sugar is often needed to bring out the full flavor of a product. I no longer add sugar to my coffee, and I think that's a mistake, because when you drink strong coffee black the flavor is too potent. I think it needs just a little bit of sugar to balance the flavor, to complete it.

"Nowadays, pastry is much more like *cuisine,* in the sense of tasting as you go along, adding a little something here, a little something there. And it's not about cakes as much as it is about desserts served on a plate. There are warm desserts, cold desserts, desserts of every texture. It's very different from the way it was ten or fifteen years ago. It has evolved a lot in that time.

"In general, I would say, cooking has deteriorated in

the quality of the available products, but it has improved in terms of working conditions and technology. The ovens are more precise. And there is the continuing evolution of the craft, as in all trades. The Ferrari only exists because others had invented the wheel, the engine, the chassis. Pastry has evolved with the aid of improvements in the refrigerator, the oven, and the sorbet machine, for example. The green-apple-and-basil sorbet would not have been possible with a classic sorbet-maker. Without a new machine called a Pacojet, it would have been too stiff.

"Cooking has also evolved because people eat less, they pay attention to their health, and they don't have as much time. They're moving too fast to eat well, and they can't have heavy desserts with a lot of cream or chocolate. And yet, if we look at the menus of fifty and sixty years ago, there were practically no desserts. Why? Because the ovens were inferior. They didn't have thermostats. They were wood or coal ovens, so they were imprecise. Also, in earlier times people would have already eaten two or three appetizers, three or four fish, and four or five meats by the end of the meal. They stayed at the table for hours. It was hard to make room for dessert. In those days the menus were impressive. And the people were like this." He holds his arms out in a ring.

"The desserts in the sixteenth century were often a basket of fruit, or a parfait—that was the beginning of the ice-cream epoch. Catherine de Médicis, of course, brought the first ice creams to France. These were light desserts. Even if it has eggs, cream, and sugar, when we eat something cold it goes down easily. Desserts have developed from there.

"Things evolve more quickly now, because there's much more communication. We travel more. We read more articles. Last week I was in Cannes, and the basil was excellent. I thought, 'I could make a cookie with basil.' Then I bought a book at the train station, and that gave me a couple of ideas about desserts made with other plants. Or if a friend is wearing a new perfume, I think, 'Ah, I can do something with whatever gives that perfume its scent.' Anything can serve as a trigger. Films, books, people."

I ask if he has been consciously inspired by architecture and the arts.

"No, but I'm very young, so I don't have much experience." He smiles. "The problem is that form is a bit trickier in pastry than in cuisine. In pastry there are fewer forms than flavors. If you're going to make a dessert with chocolate, you'll need to make a mousse of some kind. You need to *give* it a form. In cooking, truffles, carrots, chicken, and fish already have a form. Whereas vanilla, coffee, chocolate, lemon—these are flavors. And since you need to *give* them a form, that diminishes what you can do in terms of presentation. If you put it in a mold, you need to be able to extract it, so you can't use a form that is too complex. Round, pyramidical, rectangular, or square, but not with complicated details.

"In pastry, if you look at the croissant, someone

conceived of that form. For a brioche, you use a round mold, slightly channeled. *Pain au chocolat* is simply rolled dough. At Taillevent, decoration is secondary. The important thing is taste. Nonetheless, we need to think a little more, within these kinds of restraints, about the techniques of presentation. It was a pastry cook who invented the pastry bag. A young apprentice, in fact. It was late in the eighteenth or early in the nineteenth century, and he made a little paper cone, a *cornet,* and filled it with icing of some kind, and began to doodle aimlessly. The master said, 'Hey, stop fooling around!' But later he said, 'Hmm. That might actually be interesting.' The pastry bag descended from that *cornet.*"

During one dinner service I watched Debras use a small paper *cornet,* very like the one invented by the young apprentice, while preparing the *Griottes de Fougerolles en Chaud-Froid,* the dessert of marinated cherries. He began by placing two carefully formed scoops of speckled vanilla ice cream touching but off center in a plate, then poured a dark, cherry-colored sauce in the shape of a capital D around them. This semicircular ring of sauce, two fingers wide, did not touch the scoops of ice cream it contained. Debras then took up a small paper *cornet,* filled with a fluid white icing, and made a thin S, four inches wide and an inch high, within the length of the D's straight bar. With a toothpick, he then carved a tight, wavy line from left to right, passing up and down through all three lines of the broad white S. The icing tailed in the wake of the toothpick, creating a delicate pattern that suggested a lacing of white leaves against the dark sauce, or three rows of miniature, stylized whale flukes. It was one of those tricks, so simple in its execution, so difficult to describe, and so splendid in effect, that make pastry cooking so much fun to observe.

Earlier, when preparing the cherries for the dessert, Bajolle stewed them at a boil in large pans. The original flavor of the cherries, he explained, is destroyed in the cooking process, so one must know what elements compose the flavor of a cherry, and restore them. To that end, he adds vinegar, lemon extract, bitter almond, and a small amount of thyme.

I later asked Bajolle if he has been notably influenced by foreign cuisines.

"There are many interesting flavors in Italy—corn flour, polenta, fresh pasta, many things. As for Japan, sushi is not really a cuisine, but soy sauce is very interesting. Mr. Robuchon has learned a lot from Japan. I think that at a certain time he was enormously inspired by Japanese cooking. Jasmine is very interesting. And green tea. But I use very few Asian spices. At the moment, I use only coriander, with pineapple. I find the scents of most Asian spices too potent, too aggressive.

"In any case," he continued, "I think France is very complete. It has a very long history, and each region has a certain style. Many regions, like Alsace, have a foreign influence in their cuisines. The north has its beer. If you go down through the Juras, and to the Côte d'Azur, the flavors are different—apricot, almond, basil, olive oil, garlic. In the southwest, the cuisine is much more of the earth, with robust ingredients—peaches, *foie gras*, potatoes, truffle, many more root vegetables. To the northwest, of course, creams and very refined butters. But there is very good cream in Alsace as well, because the pasturage in Alsace is excellent. In France one can find many good things.

"In this trade, every day you learn something new. Like today, when Sarah made a banana cake—that might give me an idea to do something else. Or Reiko, with her Japanese desserts. That's what I find fascinating. Such understanding is limitless. All through life, you can always do something a little differently, you can always add something new."

I had heard that Robuchon goes to the market each day and selects his produce from local merchants. I asked Bajolle if he could do the same.

"Robuchon did that once," said Bajolle. "He's not going to go each day to find his fish and meat and vegetables. If he wants a certain quality of veal, he'll go to the farmer, he'll try the meat, and he'll say, 'This is good. I want it exactly like this, every time.' It is the same with fish and vegetables. You need to be able to say, 'I want this size, this quality, consistently.' When you work in the city, you need to trust the farmer, the fisherman."

How does the experience of cooking at home differ from cooking at the restaurant?

"At Taillevent, we put it in the dumbwaiter. On a trip to Brazil, for example, where I helped prepare a special meal, I was able to go out into the dining room and talk to the clients. That was wonderful. We could talk about the dishes, about how they were made, and why they were made in such a way. That was very enriching. At Taillevent, one can imagine the clients, but one does not see them. At home, it's for my children, for my wife. My daughter in particular is very enthusiastic. She always asks, 'What will you make for me to taste today?' She is always eager for new things, new associations."

I asked what he eats at home.

"It all depends on whether you have time. Simple or complicated, I always use good produce. It's not necessary to have things too complicated. If you don't have the time, you can make good, simple things. Breakfast for me is often a cup of tea or coffee and a brioche, lightly toasted, with butter and a very good jam. Or perhaps an omelet with cold ratatouille. Last week I ate a green apple for breakfast—just the apple. During the week, I eat an enormous amount, tasting all day. So on the weekend I rest my stomach. I don't eat much. Last night I ate a salad of lettuce, tomato, and beans from the garden, with a little olive oil, balsamic vinegar, salt, pepper. Simple but very good."

I asked which of his desserts have proved most popular over time.

"The oldest dessert, the most classic, is the *marquise au chocolat*. One of the most popular is certainly the *moelleux*, but it depends on whether the client has the time, for that takes ten minutes to cook. At lunch, the business clients have to leave at three o'clock. If they all arrive at the same time for lunch, as they often do, the kitchen is a *bordel*. So the client waits for the first plate, he waits for the second plate, and then he may have cheese. So, when the server asks, 'Monsieur, would you like a dessert?,' the client looks at his watch. 'Aha, quarter of three! *C'est pas possible*. Coffee!' In any case, the client may know that at Taillevent there are always petits-fours served with the coffee."

I asked him which of his desserts he prefers.

"I like them all. I like the *dacquoise* very much. The *griottes* I like less: the taste of alcohol is too strong. But Mr. Vrinat prefers to keep it on the menu, because you need desserts for all tastes. There are clients who like a strong flavor of alcohol, others who like chocolate, others who like fruit, so the menu is for everyone. The *terrine de fruits*, for example. This is a dessert with no fat, no cream, no egg whites, not much sugar. The sorbets are the same: very light and fruity. The apple-and-basil sorbet is very good and very light. That is a new association of flavors. Basil in a dessert is entirely new."

"The best meal I have ever had is my mother's *lapin à la moutarde*," Bajolle once told me. "Better than lobster, better than truffles, better than *foie gras*. I would walk many miles for that meal. You must have a good rabbit to begin with, and then it's all in the manner of preparation. My mother often looks in the oven to see how the rabbit is cooking. When it's done, she takes it out of the oven and lets it cool briefly. If you leave the rabbit in the oven, the moisture softens the skin, and it loses its delicious crust. There are countless similar details.

"Not all advances in technology have been good for cooking. Consider the thickness of a mold. Formerly, molds were very thick. The heat was well diffused, as through copper. Now it's Teflon, and the heat goes straight to the product. That's not good. The heat must gradually penetrate the product. If it gets too hot too quickly it creates a barrier, a crust. So the product does not cook as it must.

"Now we use ovens with pulsed air. The air is hot, and the hot wind dries out the food. With traditional stone ovens, it was different. When cooking bread, you washed the inside of the oven with a wet rag, and that gave it a humid atmosphere. Now it's the reverse—the oven dries out the product.

"You must always consider how things were done before, and what the result was. That's one of the great problems with machines, like the beater. The people who invented the machines didn't work with a chef or a pastry chef. They invented a machine, and the chef was obliged to alter his recipe. That's not good. It would have been better had they altered the machine. When he had no machine, the baker worked the dough like this." He mimicked the motion. "That was hard work, and the sweat of the baker would drip into the dough. They used to call that *'le goût du boulanger'* [the taste of the baker], because you could taste it faintly in the bread. So every baker's bread was a little different, even with identical ingredients. But the first machines were like that. It was a Swiss machine with arms, and it reproduced more or less the same movement. But it was very expensive. Now they no longer exist. Now the machines turn, so the effect is different, and the result is different, because dough, when it turns, heats up. In the old way, the dough did not heat up. It was only mixed, as it should be.

"The taste of bread is what? Fermentation. Wine is the fermentation of grape skins, the transformation of sugar into alcohol. The modification of things. Cheese is the transformation of milk through molds. Every cellar has a certain taste that is imparted to the cheese, that gives it its flavor. Sheep's milk, cow's milk, goat's milk—they all have a different flavor. Now there are industrial cheeses. What do they do? They taste a good artisanal cheese and say, 'Okay, this cheese has this and this and this flavor.' But when they make an industrial cheese, and pasteurize the milk, the natural flavor is completely destroyed. So afterward they add a little of this and a little of that to give flavor to the cheese.

"To see the effect of transformation, make something today, taste it, put the rest in the fridge, and taste it tomorrow. The flavors and aromas will mix and give it a different taste—sometimes better, sometimes worse. Or take bread. If you work flour, water, and yeast into dough and bake it right away, the bread will have a certain taste. Now let the dough rise, bake it, and taste it again. Very different."

I asked Bajolle about the half-bottle of wine we ordered. I told him that to our surprise we found it good but not stunning.

"The transformation of wine in the bottle is much better when there is a certain quantity," he said, echoing the sommelier. "In a small bottle, the wine is very cramped, so it develops in a certain way. And in a very big bottle, the wine is even better. It's exactly the same with bread. If you make a tiny little loaf of bread, the result is not so good. If you make a larger quantity, the transformation and the taste are much more interesting. The problem with small bottles is that people are drinking less and less, in part because they need to watch out for the police while driving. That's understandable. So you need to come in fours, and buy a bigger bottle. In any case, a wine or a dish is never perfect."

We spoke of our cheeses.

"The names are very good," he said, "but who made them? I know a *fromager* who makes even finer cheeses, but he's very expensive. I introduced him to Mr. Vrinat, who tasted his cheeses and agreed they were extraordinary. But they were very, very expensive. So Mr. Vrinat declined."

Later, I ask if he is frustrated by the transitory nature of his work.

"I am. There are dishes I've succeeded at making once, and have never been able to re-create. In that sense it's like a painting—you do it once. But the painting remains. Cooking or pastry is vapor." He grasps in the air. "So it is frustrating. But it would be less so if we had the chance to speak with the client for whom we have prepared a plate. At Taillevent, no. We put the dessert in the dumbwaiter. Earlier today, I asked a *maître d'hôtel* if a client had liked a dessert. 'Ah yes,' he told me. 'He said it was very good.' But if we don't ask, we never know.

"As I said the other day, I like what I do, but I am not passionate about it. If I could really do something, I would build something that remained, something with my hands, like a château. And make it only once. Not repeat *pêche verveine* every day, not repeat the *moelleux*, not repeat this or that. To make something once, like Mozart."

I point out that cooking professionally, with rare exceptions, is that very process of repetition.

"Exactly. That's why I would like to change professions. I have a horror of redoing always the same thing. Secondly, the fear of disappointing others is very strong in me. In the mornings, I open the restaurant. I have never been late—not once. Because it's my responsibility. If I did something more interesting for a living, I suspect I would have less fear. I'm always trying something new, so I can't be sure of the result. And yet I prefer to have the fear, and to discover something new. But the fear is terrible. When they come to Taillevent, people have high expectations. I have no right to disappoint them. I cannot."

I suggest that he is still young and could change professions.

"Yes, but the principal problem is to have a wife, two

children. Once my children are grown, if my wife works, I could change jobs. But one must pay attention to the family. One must reflect."

While he may surrender a degree of creative flexibility as a restaurant employee, there are advantages. If he had his own pastry shop, he said, he would never see his children, and he would have to work weekends. Taillevent is closed on the weekends, and he is home in the evenings for dinner.

"Taillevent is a very, very good restaurant, *une très belle maison*," he says. "It's wonderful, because with few exceptions we are able to buy the best products and equipment, and the best cooks.

"The problem with this *maison* is that Mr. Vrinat would like to be the *chef de cuisine*, he would like to be the pastry chef. Mr. Vrinat would like people to talk about Taillevent, but Taillevent, Mr. Vrinat; not Taillevent, Gilles Bajolle, Pastry Chef. When one goes to Mr. Robuchon, one eats *chez* Mr. Robuchon, because Robuchon is the chef. Here, one eats *chez* Taillevent, but Mr. Vrinat isn't the chef. Therefore, if one says, 'Ah, I've eaten very, very well,' the compliment is not for Mr. Vrinat but for the chef."

I compare it to a film production, with Vrinat as the producer.

"Yes, but *cuisine* is different," he says. "It's the chef. One man. When you go to eat *chez* Mr. Trois Gros, one thinks 'Ah, *bonjour*, Mr. Trois Gros, that was very, very good.' One forgets. One completely forgets that there are, perhaps, fifty people in the restaurant. In film, one thinks of the actors, the music, the dialogue. But in cuisine, it's 'Ah, Mr. Robuchon, Mr. Trois Gros, *formidable*.' One forgets the dishwasher, the one who did the decorations, the one who prepared the flowers. One forgets all that."

"And the owner, too," I add, "if he is not the chef."

"Exactly. But at Taillevent there is Mr. Vrinat. He doesn't want the clients to come into the kitchen. He wants them to say, 'Ah, Mr. Vrinat, it was excellent.' Several weeks ago, a client ordered a meal of nothing but desserts. He was very pleased with the result, and insisted on coming in to thank us. But this is very rare.

"I do think Mr. Vrinat is a good apprentices' master," he says. "Even if he cannot teach you, he pushes you to learn. On the one hand, it's good that he drives the restaurant to be better. He's very strong-minded; I don't know if this is natural in him, or by obligation. He is a very mysterious man. Very interesting. He's like Napoleon."

At 11:45, when we are halfway through the first two desserts, the *Moelleux au Chocolat et au Thym* arrives. A warm, vertical cylinder of baked chocolate cake, some three inches high, flanked by two delicately pointed scoops of what looks like vanilla ice cream, and an arc of warm chocolate sauce on the plate. The ice cream is infused with thyme. When I cut into the cylinder with a fork, I pierce a cell of steaming liquid chocolate sauce that runs out onto the plate, mixes with the other chocolate, and begins to melt the ice cream around its edges. The dessert is complex and delicious.

"When I was at Laurent," Bajolle later tells me, "we made a *moelleux* something like that. But the cookie was half cooked; the interior did not cook through. Then I found a recipe in a book where the pastry chef put ganache inside. But the cocoa was too strong in that recipe, so the taste was not quite right. So a little bit of each idea went into this *moelleux*. One day we tasted chocolate and thyme together, for tasting an infusion, and when I saw that the thyme went well with the chocolate, I decided to make thyme ice cream to serve with the *moelleux*. And yet, if we had only the *moelleux* and the ice cream, the dessert would somehow be incomplete. So we added the sauce to the plate, which is chocolate and lemon. Lemon goes well with thyme and with chocolate. This was five or six years ago, and since then it has become a classic dessert at Taillevent.

"To select the chocolate, we tasted different varieties from different manufacturers. Nowadays, chocolate is made in huge factories. If you want to make something more personal, you need to take different chocolates, taste them, and mix them yourself. You'll find your own mix, to your taste. In the *marquise au chocolat* there are five different chocolates. There are four in the *moelleux*.

"Chocolate is like wine," says Bajolle. "Every year it's different. Sometimes the chocolate is more acidic. Where the cocoa is grown, it may have been more humid, or more sunny. The environment may change in other ways. Later, the chocolate maker will taste the various chocolates and say, 'Ah, this year I need to take a little more of this chocolate, and a little less of that variety, to arrive at the same particular taste.' The quality of the sugar will also have its effect. It's very, very difficult to have the palate necessary to reproduce the same quality and flavor of chocolate year after year."

Sumerians favored thyme for its medicinal properties, and the Egyptians included it in their spice chest for embalming. Considered an aphrodisiac by the ancients, the herb was sacrificed to Venus. Though Bajolle's dessert may be unprecedented, he is not the first to marry thyme with a sweet; Aristophanes praised a drink flavored with thyme and figs. In the first few minutes A.D., the manger for the newborn Jesus is said to have been padded with a rustic bedding that included thyme straw. Whether this was by chance or parental intent is unclear, although thyme was popularly believed to have protective qualities. If we discount the ambient scent of the livestock, thyme may thus have been the first earthly smell to greet the Son of Man. The Romans believed thyme to be a cure for depression and a dietary source of physical bravery— the Latin equivalent of Jack Daniel's at Gettysburg. One imagines trembling legionnaires munching down the stuff by the fistful as the beer-emboldened Germans swept down upon them—the only foe, apart from the Picts of northern Britain, who consistently sent the Romans packing. In 9 A.D., when General Varus lost three of Rome's best legions (more than sixteen thousand men) to the Germans, together with the golden eagles that served as their standards—a blow that put Augustus off his food for a week—one wonders if Varus simply ran out of thyme.

Near the end of my stay at Taillevent, I ask Bajolle where he thinks cooking will go in the next ten or twenty years.

"We've talked about the fact that cooking has become lighter," he says. "The portions have diminished, and our respect for the products has grown. I think we'll go even further in mixing cuisines. French—Italian, Italian—Japanese, etc. We'll take ideas right and left."

"A global cuisine," I suggest.

"And it's too bad," he says, nodding. "It's really too bad. In the old days, the cheeses were different in each region. We no longer invent cheeses. In those times, when people didn't move as much, each cook or farmer stayed in his little spot and made something very personal. Now, if one stays personal, one doesn't evolve. Or, rather, the evolution will be more and more uniform, in the sense that we will not create things that are truly unique. We'll steal ideas here and there for making new combinations. Why are we no longer inventing warm drinks, for example? How long has tea existed? How long has coffee existed, or chocolate? We no longer invent infusions. Why not vanilla? And we no longer invent flavors. We mix a little vanilla, strawberry, cardamom, anise—and we call that a new flavor. But truly fundamental flavors, no. And they do exist.

"One must understand that cooking takes time, close observation, reflection, and a good palate," he says. "You cannot hurry; you must know how to wait for the correct result. And since eating involves all five senses—sight, smell, touch, taste, even hearing—you need to keep all these in mind as you prepare a dish. Ideally, you will stimulate all the senses in a good meal. The food must look beautiful to the eye, and there must be delicious smells, and different textures—smooth, crisp, warm, cool. When you make a dish, everything is important. Even the sounds of different foods should be considered, like the crunch of something crisp under the teeth."

After the *fantaisie*, to my taste, the *marquise* edges out the *moelleux* as the second-best dessert in Bajolle's repertoire. One afternoon before our meal, I help him prepare it, mixing the different chocolates in precise doses and beating scores of egg whites into drifts of foam. I scoop the blended mixture into six glass terrines, level them neatly with an icing knife, and rap the terrines firmly on the counter to encourage the bubbles to rise. Then we cover them with plastic wrap and put them in the fridge to chill. Later, when the first order comes in for the dessert, Debras removes a mold from its terrine, cuts a perfect slice a third of an inch thick, and lays it carefully in the center of a dessert plate. He pulls a plastic squirt bottle of pale-green pistachio sauce from a fridge under the counter and creates a shallow, circular green sea around the chocolate island. It is a beautiful green, paler and more exotic than pea soup, and it looks splendid beside the chocolate. Visually, it is one of the simplest and most attractive of all the desserts. The sauce, a *crème anglaise* infused with pistachio paste, must be a certain consistency, Debras explains. I squirt a dash of it into the middle of a clean plate and tilt the plate at a slight angle, allowing the sauce to run slowly down its face. I tip the plate back and forth, running my finger through it, until I am clear on the correct consistency. The sauce is sublime on its own, if you like pistachio, and with the *marquise* it is better. The *marquise* itself is what cocoa beans dream of becoming. More dense and silken than any mousse, richer than fudge but not cloying, it is firm enough to hold its form and yet melts on the tongue. There is not the faintest fudgelike graininess, or the stickiness of chocolate bars, or any quality of foam. It is light but airless, creamy, and firm.

Months later, in California, I attempt to reproduce Bajolle's *marquise*. I am forced to deviate from his recipe almost immediately, since our local chocolatier, though excellent, does not have the precise chocolates called for. I can't find the pistachio paste in time, so I infuse ground, fresh pistachios and strain them through ten or twelve layers of cheesecloth. And the other ingredients, even if of the best available quality, are American, not French. Bajolle once told me that he would happily give any of his recipes to anyone who asked. "Unless it is made with the exact same ingredients, in the exact same way, the result will be very, very different. It may be very good, but it will be different. If I go to Brazil, for example, I will take as many of my own ingredients as possible. As for the ingredients I need to find there, they will all be different in some way. Cream, for example. The cows, their diet, the way they're raised: it all affects the flavor of the cream. So I will taste them—the cream, the butter, the eggs, everything—and alter the recipe as necessary to reproduce the taste I'm after. The recipe is a start, but it is nearly meaningless without the palate and technique of the chef."

In any event, I set out my faux American ingredients, with the sense that I may as well try to make a *marquise* with hair gel and sawdust. Nonetheless, I pull on my white cooking jacket and plunge in. We are expecting friends for supper, an Italian sculptor and his wife, who is French Canadian and an excellent, intuitive cook, and I want to make something they will enjoy, something that may remind them, however distantly, of Europe or Quebec. Melting and blending the five chocolates, beating the huge bowl of whites, working steadily but not too fast, I quickly become utterly absorbed.

Usually, when I cook, I am distracted. I am often tense, and frustrated by the fact that the peeler or small whisk cannot be found. Why are these things never, ever in their proper places? They're dirty, of course, the whisk crusted with goo under a pile of debris in the sink. I scrub it furiously, resentfully. I feel some misgiving about the dish, or dishes, I am putting together.

What is going wrong? Why can't I re-create that simple sauce, a sauce I've made so many times before? What a dull combination, I think. Yet another thing I do poorly. And why, for God's sake, can't these people shut up and get out of the kitchen? In response to all this, and to make myself more sociable, I usually pour myself a double gin-and-tonic, maybe two. This loosens my cooking artificially; I add more olive oil, more garlic, more of anything. Sometimes that is all for the good. Often it isn't, but by that point I'm too anesthetized to care.

On this particular afternoon, the cooking is calming in itself. The green bottle of gin, reclining in the freezer, does not even occur to me. I find myself inside the ingredients, smitten by the volume and the purity of the colors. Outwardly quiet, I begin to feel supremely happy, even ecstatic. I am relaxed but full of energy. Wow, I think. What is this? I ride it through the afternoon, sinking steadily deeper into the small steps, one after another, relishing the preparation as one relishes the finished dish itself. In the end, the dessert is fantastic. Even I am forced to admit it. It worked. It is the *marquise au chocolat*. The spirit of Bajolle made it through.

Le Départ

At 12:05, a waiter we have not seen delivers two glasses of house cognac to our table. We ask if we can pay our respects to the kitchen, but the cooks are long gone—the kitchens are spotless, deep in shadow. Downstairs, the range is still warm to the touch. The cooks are crossing Paris on their motorcycles, along the quays or the *périphérique,* the Paris beltway. Some of them have repaired to the café at the end of the rue Lamennais for a *demi* of Stella Artois or a 1664. They are dehydrated from a day at the stoves, and their legs and backs and feet are tired. Some of them have new cuts on their hands, hastily bandaged, or new burns on their forearms, ugly and purple, chafing under the sleeves of their jackets. For fourteen hours of work in a day, five days a week, they will earn on average a monthly salary in the neighborhood of twelve thousand francs—about two thousand dollars. This breaks down to an hourly wage of about seven dollars. A senior cook like Guibert will earn somewhat more than this, a *commis* proportionately less. For most of them, living in Paris, this is barely enough to make ends meet. But they have eaten well enough in the refectory, and they work in the best place in town, and if they keep at it nearly all of them will have bright futures in the kitchens of France.

I ask for the bill, and when the waiter returns with it, as I sip the cognac, we chat with him, about his family, his twelve-year-old daughter who has grown too fast. Like his colleagues it seems, he is a professional, a career waiter. Very likely, he will work here until he retires. Like all of them, he has a warm and gracious manner. It is late on a weeknight, at the end of a long shift. He is surely tired, but he shows no sign of it. By appearances, he would be happy to chat into the morning. He reminds me of the figure in that short story of Hemingway's, the bartender who understood the elderly insomniac who stayed too late at the bar. Our captain and the staff of our section have vanished. The dining room is all but abandoned. The tables are cleared. You can almost hear the clocks. It is Bastille Day.

I look at the bill. It is just over two thousand francs. That is a pretty sum, but at this moment it seems like a bargain. The *service compris* (service charge) of 15 percent aside, I leave another 10 percent in cash. I worry that perhaps that's not enough, that they won't know how grateful we are for their kindness, professional and trained though it may be. On the other hand, I do not want them to feel that I am paying them off, as it were, for their good grace. It's a fine balance. We are only two foreign faces in an endless stream, and none of the servers are here as volunteers. None of them, either, are eating at Taillevent or its like with any regularity, if at all. I remember all too well what it was like to wait tables, and the irony that we have eaten a week's salary for one of the cooks is not lost on us. I leave a two-hundred-franc note and hope it serves.

At 12:20, not quite four hours after sitting down, we stand from the table. Anticipating our movement, the waiter sweeps the table away from us with a bow. My head swims. My legs are stiff, and the sensation of mass and density in my midsection is startling. I have reached a capacity that I have never before known. I could consume not one more drop or crumb. I am physically discomfited by the load, I realize upon standing. I've overdone it. This sensation only increases as we begin to walk. Good God, I think, a pinprick of anxiety rising through the meal's euphoria. Can you actually injure yourself with a meal?

In a neighboring section, a lone French couple on a banquette has outlasted us. They speak in low tones, leaning in toward the table and each other, nodding, sipping from small glasses. Their check lies on the table. As we ease around the bend into the hallway, accompanied by the waiter, the coat checker appears with a small gold box—the petits-fours we asked to take home—and a clean copy of our menu as a keepsake. As she hands these articles to us, thanks us, and wishes us a good night, she bestows upon us the smile she smiled on our arrival. The smile for the important, the beautiful, and the beloved, the smile she would give to Chirac, or to Adjani, or to a train mechanic from Le Havre, should he appear one evening in a threadbare jacket and indelibly black fingernails scrubbed raw, with a pocket full of neatly folded cash and his wife of thirty-five years.

In April, a Swiss executive flew fifty-five friends and colleagues first class from Zürich to Paris for dinner at Taillevent. There are 120 seats in the house on two floors, including private rooms upstairs, but he wanted the place for himself, so he paid the difference. After dinner, he put his crowd up at Le Bristol, and flew them back to Zürich the next day. The price tag for this display of power eludes precise calculation, but it falls well into six figures U.S. The tab at Taillevent, with wine and the empty tables, must have exceeded forty thousand dollars, and that is a conservative estimate. If he shot the moon with the wine list, he could have spent three or four times that. Swiss moguls aside, Taillevent regularly serves many of the wealthiest and most powerful people in France. They also serve the farmer, the young couple, the bookkeeper, the foreigner out on a limb. And to the best of their ability, as far as I can tell, they try to give to each of them—be he spellbound or indifferent, meek or bombastic—the identical experience. Or, rather, the experience each of them hoped for. If there is a kind of miracle at work at Taillevent, it is not so much in the kitchens, as extraordinary as the food truly is. More than the food, to my amazement, it is the service.

The *maître d'hôtel* who greeted us holds the door. Beside him is the last waiter, the gentleman who brought us our check. After an exchange of thanks, they wish us good night and we step out into the street. We stand there for a moment, our eyes adjusting to the darkness of the rue Lamennais, as the door closes inaudibly behind us.

The midnight air is cool, and taxis can be heard passing on the rue Balzac. It smells like Paris late at night, when the traffic has ebbed. Paris smells best in the autumn—in October, before dawn, after a rain—but even on this early Bastille Day in midsummer, the city smells of stone, of finished masonry and cobbles, a damp, clean, faintly mineral smell not unlike that of a quarry. There is a hint of a cigarette burning somewhere far upwind, and there is something inexplicably fresh, a scent like wet gravel and chestnut trees. There must be a square not far off. The smell of trees is strengthened by what must be farm and woodland, for a fresh breeze is blowing gently across the city from the west, rinsing the boulevards of exhaust. Suddenly there is a note of something savory and pungent cooking in an apartment overhead. Smelling the scent of a meal cooking in a strange apartment late at night is like hearing the sounds of lovemaking through closed shutters in a hotel courtyard. The passing revelation of the intimate life of strangers binds us to them; we perceive the span of their brief lives in an instant. We are awed by their ability to love and to eat, to indulge a mortal appetite on so slender a precipice. In front of Taillevent, before we turn down the sidewalk, I pause and glance back through the glass door. Shadows move vaguely at the end of the corridor. The door is shut, the pane is darkened, but within, the golden lights still burn.

L'Envoi

I went to my nearest good chocolatier and showed her Bajolle's recipe. Together, we tried our best to approximate the chocolates he calls for—and that is what I used. But if you have to rely on what's available at your supermarket I have worked out an alternative that promises to give good results.

The Marquise

(For a 1-quart Pyrex loaf pan)

½ cup sugar

7 extra large egg yolks

2 extra large eggs

9 tablespoons (1 stick and 1 tablespoon) butter (unsalted)

1½ cups heavy cream

1¾ ounces (¼ cup) unsweetened powdered cocoa

9 ounces chocolate, comprised of:

      3½ ounces *maitre chocolatier* chocolate

      3½ ounces *cacao pur pate* (unsweetened dark)

L'Envoi

½ ounce *caraque* chocolate

1 ounce extra bitter chocolate

(These are all manufactured by Vahlrona—if unavailable, ask your local *chocolatier* for the nearest equivalents.) Or, if those varieties prove elusive, as they did for me:

6 ounces sweetened chocolate

3½ ounces unsweetened dark chocolate

Preparation

Melt the hard chocolate and butter together in a double boiler until fluid. Remove from the heat. While that's cooling, beat the cream until stiff and set it aside. Beat the whole eggs, the yolks, and the sugar until well mixed. When the chocolate is cool to the touch, add it to the egg and sugar mixture and beat another minute or so. Now add the cocoa powder slowly and beat four or five minutes, until it is thoroughly blended. Finally, gently fold the beaten cream into the chocolate with a spatula. Try your best not to deflate the mixture, but keep folding until the color is uniform. There should be no streaks or marbling.

Pour the mixture into the Pyrex loaf pan, filling it completely. Use a frosting knife to level the surface to the rim of the pan. Thump the bottom of the pan firmly on a wooden counter or cutting board a few times to remove any air bubbles. Cover the pan with plastic wrap and refrigerate it overnight, or for at least eight hours, before serving. The Marquise will last three days if refrigerated.

The Pistachio Sauce

½ cup minus 1 tablespoon sugar

3½ ounces pure pistachio paste (unsweetened) such as
that produced by Fabbri

5 extra large egg yolks

2¼ cups whole milk

I failed to find the pistachio paste in time to serve with my first attempt, so I made a pistachio extract using fresh pistachios. This was time-consuming and the sauce was not as intense as one made with paste, so I strongly suggest finding a can of good paste before you start.

Preparation

Bring the milk to a low boil, add the pistachio paste, and stir it off the heat until thoroughly dissolved. Allow the milk to cool. Beat the sugar into the yolks and transfer to a medium-sized pot. Pour the cooled pistachio milk slowly over the yolk mixture, stirring constantly. Continuing to stir with a flat-tipped spatula, cook over a low flame (at 82°C, or 180°F, ideally) for about a minute. Keep scraping the thickening crème off the bottom of the pot as you stir. As with any *crème anglaise*, if you overcook it and the eggs curdle, you will have to start again.

The best test for readiness, according to Bajolle, is as follows: Dip a flat wooden spatula into the crème, then pull it out and hold the blade perpendicular to the floor.

Run a fingertip lengthwise through the middle of the blade. If the crème runs down across the finger streak, it is still too thin. If the finger streak remains, it is ready.

Pass the crème through a fine cheesecloth or *chinois* and refrigerate. Bajolle stores it in a plastic squeeze bottle, which makes serving easier. The *crème à la pistache* is shorter-lived than the Marquise, lasting only twenty-four hours refrigerated.

To Serve

Dip the bottom and sides of the loaf pan in hot water, then flip it carefully onto a plate or tray large enough to hold the Marquise flat. Ease the pan up and off the Marquise. If it clings, repeat the hot water dip. If you do this step earlier in the day, to save time, cover the Marquise completely with plastic wrap, leaving no air pockets, and re-refrigerate.

When it comes time to serve, cut slices from the Marquise ⅓ inch thick. For one serving, lay two slices together, the longest side of each touching in the center of a full-sized, room-temperature plate. Extended air exposure is death to such a dish, so rewrap the remainder carefully in plastic and return quickly to the fridge. Ideally, the Marquise should be cut into slices mere minutes before serving. If you prepare it this way, the dessert will be cool but not cold—the ideal temperature—when it arrives at the table. Finally, pool sauce around the Marquise to cover the plate's inner diameter, creating a chocolate island in a pistachio sea.

For the sake of accuracy, here are the ingredients in their original weights, as provided by Bajolle.

The Marquise

(For 6 terrines of 1 liter each)

675 grams (24 ounces) of sugar

45 egg yolks

15 whole eggs

1500 grams (53 ounces) butter (unsalted)

2 liters (68 fluid ounces, or 2 quarts and ½ cup) whole cream

300 grams (10.5 ounces) powdered cocoa, unsweetened

1500 grams (53 ounces) of chocolate, comprised of:

> 600 grams (21 ounces) *maitre chocolatier* chocolate
>
> 600 grams (21 ounces) *cacao pur pate* (unsweetened dark)
>
> 100 grams (3.5 ounces) *caraque* chocolate
>
> 200 grams (7 ounces) extra bitter chocolate

Or, if those varieties prove elusive:

> 1000 grams (35 ounces) sweetened chocolate
>
> 500 grams (17.5 ounces) unsweetened dark chocolate

The Pistachio Sauce

180 grams (6.5 ounces) sugar

180 grams (6.5 ounces) pure pistachio paste (unsweetened) such as that produced by Fabbri

10 egg yolks

1 liter (1 quart and ¼ cup) whole milk